TWO
HUNDRED YEARS
OF CHARLESTON COOKING

Published in Columbia, South Carolina, during the one hundred and seventy-fifth anniversary of the establishment of the University of South Carolina and the two hundredth anniversary of the establishment of the United States of America.

CORNER OF COURTYARD BETWEEN THE PIRATE HOUSE AND MRS. WOODWARD'S SMALL HOUSE WHICH WAS BUILT BY MRS. RHETT

TWO HUNDRED YEARS OF CHARLESTON COOKING

RECIPES GATHERED BY
Blanche S. Rhett

AND EDITED BY
Lettie Gay

WITH AN INTRODUCTION
AND EXPLANATORY MATTER BY
Helen Woodward

AND A NEW FOREWORD BY
Elizabeth Hamilton

UNIVERSITY OF
SOUTH CAROLINA PRESS

Columbia, South Carolina

Manufactured in the United States of America
ISBN 0-87249-346-6 (hardcover)
0-87249-348-2 (paperback)

CONTENTS

Foreword by Elizabeth Verner Hamilton .... *(vii)*
"How This Book Came To Be" by Helen Woodward ix
"Tried and Found Good" by Lettie Gay xv
SOUPS AND CANAPÉS 1
SHELLFISH AND FISH 17
PILAUS, EGG DISHES AND OTHER MAIN DISHES 43
POULTRY AND DRESSINGS 66
STUFFINGS 80
MEATS 89
SWEET POTATOES, RICE AND GREEN VEGETABLES 101
SALADS AND RELISHES 121
BREADS 143
CAKES AND CANDIES 166
DESSERTS 223
BEVERAGES 273
INDEX 283

FOREWORD

THE PRESIDENT of the University of South Carolina is a gourmet and a Charlestonian. He has long wished to have this treasury of Charleston cuisine back in print. The University of South Carolina Press, used to scholarly tomes, has just realized the cultural value of a cook-book and has asked me to write a foreword.

"200 Years of Charleston Cooking," now for the ease of librarians, who will catalog it, replicated (the word is the learned editor's, not mine) under the easier to find title *Two Hundred Years of Charleston Cooking,* was first published in 1930, reprinted twice by 1931 and was slightly revised in 1934. This is not the revised copy. All the coy, I-would-if-I-could comments of Mrs. Woodward about the addition of spirits, or the lack of them, these being Prohibition times, are left intact, as you will see for yourself.

This is a very useful book for today's gourmets who like to get into the kitchen themselves.

The good casserole dishes are here because of the Charleston habit of serving a properly balanced dinner of soup, rice and gravy, meat, two vegetables and a dessert at two or preferably 3 o'clock. Traditionally, this was cooked and served by a very good cook, who would also make a casserole to be popped into the oven for supper, which Charlestonians do not like to eat until after it is "good dark," and they've never liked the idea of help sitting around waiting to go home and creating a tension thereby. In the winter, although it gets dark earlier than it does in summer, supper is still informal and moveable, and (except for certain Seated-Butler-Dinners) servantless. Even in the old days when the kitchen was buzzing with many helpers, the lady of the house usually made the desserts (in the pantry). And here we find a definitely English tradition. Prune whip, or apricot whip with a boiled custard *(crème Anglaise),* fruit cakes and such marvels as made-ahead soufflés and fig ice-cream. By the way, Mrs. Simonds' daughter says that the ice-cream should only have one cup of custard and the rest should be rich cream. It is just as delicious when it is made with peaches.

Although the nineteen-twenties when these receipts were collected, were opulent times in the rest of the country, they were comparatively difficult times in Charleston. Our gaiety was the rueful cheerfulness of self-respect with heads held high. As it was, a lot of our entertaining was making-do with indifferent ingredients and insufficient help, seasoning both with laughter and good spirits. As a consequence, the Depression of the thirties was not as difficult for us as it was for most of the rest of the country. We had been schooled in hard times and smugly admired our ability to enjoy ourselves at home.

A Charlestonian hardly knows whether she has used the word "receipt" or the more standard modern word "recipe." Let me quote Louise Kerr, who wrote the verse introductions to that wonderful stand-by, *Charleston Receipts,*

> The word RECEIPT's been handed down
> For Generations. Its renown
> Is well established. RECIPE
> From scholarship to pendantry
> Has now evolved. However, we
> Can use them interchangeably.

Of course the French word is recette, and the people who first used them called them receipts, and so did their descendants who turned them over to their friend, Blanche Salley Rhett. It is indeed to Mrs. Rhett, Mrs. Goodwyn Rhett, and her popularity that we are indebted for this collection. Helen Woodward introduced the book and individual receipts with an outsider's inevitable misunderstanding. And Lettie Gay corrected measurements, and sometimes changed them beyond recognition, so some credit for the book undoubtedly is due them. But you would not be holding this book in your hands had not

Mrs. Rhett's wide circle of friends and admirers (she was both beautiful and generous) come forward with their treasures.

Some of the receipts came from old unpublished or out of print collections saved in plantation kitchens from time out of mind. One of these collections was owned by the family of Bossis Plantation, passed down from mother to daughter. It was Miss Elizabeth Harleston's notebook. "Two Hundred Years" leans heavily on this collection, which has never been published. Miss Harleston's great-niece, Mary Leize Simons, and *her* daughter, Mary Leize Street, are both frequently quoted, and many of the receipts are also attributed to the plantation, *Bossis*.

Another source is *The Carolina Housewife, or House and Home of a Lady of Charleston,* Charleston, S. C. 1847. Like Mrs. Woodward, my husband and I lived in Paris for years. When we came home, we found that *The Carolina Housewife* had been reprinted. Miss Rutledge, the modest author who had published it without a signature, had lived abroad for several years and was sharing both common household knowledge and receipts she had gleaned in her travels. Her book makes marvelous reading. Glance at her seasonings. They are what we have been brought up on! Compare them to, say, Fanny Farmer. They sound much more like *The French Chef.*

Miss Rutledge tells how to cook tomatoes; how to preserve them; how to make tomato paste and how to serve tomatoes in salads. But the encyclopedia says they were not in general use in the United States (except for New Orleans) until almost the beginning of this century.

One of the most valuable things about "Two Hundred Years" is that it gives us many receipts for tomato dishes. Here is a baked shrimp casserole, a tomato sauce for fish and the superb red rice so much missed by Charlestonians away from home. Tomatoes aren't over-used either. Look at the restraint in Mrs. William Hutchinson's Cocktail Sauce for Shrimp.

Not only did my husband and I live in France, we lived in Cuba as well, and discovered that many of our Charleston rice dishes are like Cuban dishes, which are a combination of Spanish and African themes. *Arroz con pollo* is a chicken pilau, and there is a close relationship between *Moros y Cristianos* and "Hopping John" (pronounced Hoppin' John). They are plantation fare. Rice and beans make, as vegetarians and health food fans know, a complete protein. So a legume and rice was cheap good food for field hands. Some say it was brought into the house on New Year's Day as an act of humility to guarantee good luck for the ensuing year. We always served it in Washington at a New Year's Day party that lasted all day long and gathered together devotees of the dish and people who had never heard of it, but who became partial to it. Some people serve it at the stroke of midnight. When it is served as a left-over it is called Skip-In-Jenny.

Lettie Gay, the dietitian who tested the recipes in her New York laboratory, says of this dish, "We were able to get the cow peas (which look far more like beans than peas!). For our taste the dish seemed a bit flavorless. . . ." and Mrs. Woodward suggests that black beans could be used. Heresy! No South Carolinian would stand for that (But *Moros y Cristianos* is a combination of black beans and white rice). What Miss Gay didn't know, but what every Cuban, French or Charleston cook knows automatically, without having to be told by the receipt, which is used only for proportions, is that one puts in onions and a bay leaf, parsley and thyme—a *bouquet garni,* or strains a peppery, garlicky *sofrito* into the beans (or the peas), and then the dish is far from flavorless.

You will find many wonderful things to do with rice in "Two Hundred Years." But don't look for rice pudding. The very idea of sweets with rice upsets Charlestonians who take rice very seriously. Our late beloved historian and wag, Sam Stoney, used to ask the hoary old riddle, "Why is a Charlestonian like a Chinaman?" "Because he eats rice and worships his ancestors," you would reply on cue. "It used to be that way," Sam would agree, "but nowadays the question should be, What's the difference between a Charlestonian and a Chinaman? And the answer is, of course, A Chinaman lives on rice and worships his ancestors, but a Charlestonian lives on his ancestors and worships rice."

Since it was the lady of the house who made the desserts, here we find most careful measurements. There are only a few receipts for pies. Pie crust doesn't turn out very well in "giffy" weather, for flour, even flour stored in a heated house, absorbs moisture. Desserts made with lady fingers, sponge cake, whipped cream, soufflés and Charlottes, turn out much better in Charleston's humid climate. Here is also that beloved dish, Ambrosia, made of cut-up oranges, bananas and coconut, the favorite after a heavy Sunday dinner.

But times have changed. And along with the change has come a cooking spree. All sorts of people turn out to have great talents who would never have dreamed of going into a kitchen a generation ago. There is a charming story that tells about how people used to feel about their kitchens. A young Charleston bride, whose husband was overseas in service—this must be a World War I vintage story—decided to move back to her parents' home, be patriotic and rent her own house. The Navy wife who came to rent it was the ideal tenant. She loved the antique furniture, the beautiful rugs, and her cultivated tone of voice convinced the daughter and her mother that she spoke the truth when she said it was just like home.

But the next day she called up and said rather sharply, the house was lovely, but something would have to be done about the kitchen. There was a shocked silence at the other end of the line and finally the mother's voice said, "You *went* into the kitchen?"

Nowadays lots of people all over the world go into the kitchen. Nancy Astor once washed the dishes after a Sunday night supper at 38 Tradd St. with my mother; and Lady Berlin, née Rothschild, helped my husband cook his famous *soufflé au grand marnier* at 3 Water Street.

Thus, Charleston cuisine is a combination of international influences and very strictly local prejudices. Charlestonians frequently don't know which is which. Don't talk to a Charlestonian about sweet rice and don't talk to him either about grits, unless you are on your way to the grocery store. One buys grits, cooks it and the result is *hominy*. One can have hominy every day of the year for breakfast and have it for supper, too. Since it has a very bland taste it has to have something exciting to accompany it. Bacon, ham, pickled fish row, shrimp, cod-fish cakes, hogshead cheese. It is not unlike the Italian dish *polenta*. Charlestonians would understand perfectly the story about the family so poor that they could only buy one red herring. They tied it on a string hung from the ceiling and just passed it over the polenta. In our family we are also very fond of kidney stew, and hominy, for breakfast.

Of course the favorite of all breakfasts is shrimp. Many people prefer to stay in town all summer in order to enjoy the fresh little creek shrimp. The smaller the better. These are nowadays frozen when in season and kept in the deep freeze. One local method is to take off the heads, pile them into a milk carton, fill it with water and put it into the freezer. But a better way is to put the shrimp immediately on flat cookie sheets, slip the whole sheet into a bag, freeze them, slip them off the cookie sheet, tie the bag up tightly. This gives the advantage, when you want to use them, of your being able to take out a few at a time, instead of having to thaw the whole carton. A few shrimp in a sauce for flounder is a gourmet's delight; a few shrimp added to gumbo, especially if you have saved the shrimp water and used it for stock, change an everyday dish into a marvelous one, and shrimp water added to an ordinary can of tomato soup makes it a *bisque.*

Of course Charleston's eating habits have had a great influence on "soul food." Okra, bell peppers, rice and chicken dishes, the tomato dishes have been the staples of black and white households. In "Porgy and Bess," the men were fishing when they were caught out in the storm, for without fish Catfish Row would have been hungry indeed. The whole city depended on the "mosquito fleet" that brought in fresh fish, daily. The miracle of refrigeration is strictly of our own times.

But look! Here is Ethel Norvell's sweet potato pone, and Mary Leize Simons' and Ottie Ball's, each from a different plantation. And here is fruit cake, and wine jelly by Martha Laurens Patterson, Miss Virginia Porcher of Ophir Plantation's pumpkin, Miss Georgia Porter's Lemon pudding and Heningham Ellet Smith's Chocolate Sponge (Mrs. Woodward slipped up here on the sex of Mrs. J. J. Pringle Smith of Middleton Place). Here are several receipts that Miss Leize Dawson used at the Villa Margherita, the famous inn she ran for years. And here is Alicia Rhett Mayberry's Lady Baltimore Cake which used to be sold at the Ladies Exchange.

What is conspicuously lacking are receipts for game, which was a vital part of Low Country fare. We feel sure that the original collection Mrs. Rhett made must have contained many that were discarded. Look at the hands-off way Miss Gay reports the receipts for Cooter Soup, and her treatment of that wonderful venison pâté.

By request, I have done some research on receipts for game. Here are two additional receipts for game, and one for fish.

My research turned up an almost universal problem. These days when a hunter or fisherman brings home a prize, he is greeted with cries of dismay rather than acclaimed the noble huntsman and provider.

When we lived in Arkansas, we had a landlady who taught me an invaluable lesson. She was killing a chicken and I must have reacted as most of us do today. Plastic-wrapped offerings in the supermarket have conditioned us to squeamishness as to the origins of food. Dissection in biology class is apt to be remembered with horror, so we have little to fall back on. And then, besides, I had been brought up in the Charleston *mystique* that the more helpless a girl appears the more appealing and charming she is. My neighbor looked at me with scorn and said, "I figure if anybody can do it, I can do it."

Armed with this attitude and faced with a limp wild duck, one proceeds as follows:

Cut off the head with a sharp knife. Snap off the feet at the first joint and cut off the wing tips. Do not wet the feathers. Pluck it dry. The feathers are so beautiful you will want to save them all, but press on with the job in hand. When the outside feathers are all plucked off, you will find that the duck is covered with down. Remove the down by singeing the bird over a flame. Then pull out all the pin feathers that remain. A knife blade held against the thumb is useful. Next, with a sharp knife cut a hole beneath the tail and pull out the insides. Draw them out gently. Then, with a finger, remove the craw from the neck. Wash the bird inside and out, under the faucet. If you can, be brave, and rescue the heart, gizzard, and liver. Put them in the icebox, but don't forget them. I saw a teacher in the amphitheatre of the Cordon Bleu school in Paris do the most wonderful things with them. Then make a stock with the wing tips and the neck, seasoning it highly with carrots, celery, parsley, thyme, peppercorns, a small onion, and a clove of garlic. Cooked in the pressure cooker for twenty minutes, at least, this will give you the stock you'll need for the gravy.

Squeeze and rub an orange over the outside of the duck and thoroughly salt and pepper the cavity. Put two or three sections of orange in the cavity and add a small onion stuck with two cloves. These are to be discarded before you serve the duck. Put it into a pan. Set the oven at 300°. Let the duck cook for forty minutes, then turn the oven down as low as you can and let the duck cook for two hours. Or, you can set the oven at 400°, let the duck cook twenty minutes in the hot oven and then turn it down to 300° for forty minutes. With this method you must baste to keep the duck from drying out. As it browns, prick the skin with a fork and with a syringe scoop up the fat in the pan and douse the bird with it, repeating the process every ten or fifteen minutes. Meanwhile, put a little fat from the roaster into a frying pan. When it is hot, add the chopped-up liver, gizzard, and heart. Keep the flame high, turn frequently and then sprinkle with flour to which salt and pepper have been added, and stir rapidly to brown the flour without burning it. Squeeze over this an orange, and keep stirring. Then add the strained stock from your pressure cooker. Max Bugnaud, our teacher in Paris, who taught the French Chef—used to always put a chicken bouillon cube, in Paris called Poule-au-Pot, in almost all his sauces and gravies, but when you do this be careful lest you get too much salt from the very salty cube. When the duck is done (it should be tender and succulent), take it out of the oven and keep it warm. Pour most of the fat out of the roaster. Then return it to the top of the stove and pour the gravy into it, swishing it around so as to deglaze the roaster and get into the gravy every rich brown blob of goodness. Put this gravy into a separate gravy bowl to be served over the fluffy white rice which you have been cooking on the back of the stove. Many people like wild rice with game, but we find that with a good gravy white rice is preferable. Curried fruit goes well with the duck—and a casserole of mushrooms.

There is an alternate method that claims that the ducks are simply waltzed through the kitchen and put on the table after only a very few minutes in a very, very hot oven. The meat is still bright red. The success of this method depends on having the duck at room temperature before you begin, and in making all sauces and gravies well ahead, and serving at once.

Also, be warned, you must either cook the bird until it is very well done, and in that case the longer and slower the juicier, or very fast. Halfway between will yield a very tough, sinewy bird.

Marsh Hens

This fishy bird presents a problem, but cooked properly and served on points of toast with broiled mushrooms and cheney briar it is enough to set the most fastidious of gourmets talking for years. If you can't find cheney briar, fresh asparagus will do.

You don't pluck a marsh hen, you peel it. The skin, feathers and all, comes off like a glove. Since the birds are quite small, this feature is a big help. You'll need at least one bird to a serving. Cut off the head and the feet. At the neck, cutting under the skin with a sharp knife, start peeling. The skin will come right on off, down the legs and completely off in one piece. Then draw the birds, remove the craw and soak them overnight in water to cover them to which a tablespoon of vinegar has been added. The birds have a heavy, disagreeable fishy smell and the idea is to get rid of this. The next day wash them under running water and soak them again in water and vinegar while you make the preparations to cook them.

You'll need a pound of red onions. Slice them. Melt two tablespoons of margarine in an iron skillet. Add the onions. Cover the pan and turn the heat down as low as possible. Cook the onions very, very slowly until they literally melt. You'll find they have a sweet taste and have lost all their onion-y characteristics. An hour, or an hour and a half is required. Don't hurry this process. Low, slow heat is essential. Next, add a bay leaf, half a teaspoon of thyme, a tablespoon of chopped parsley, another tablespoon of chopped celery leaves, another tablespoon of finely chopped celery, use generously your bottle of Italian seasoning, or the Bouquet Garni, add a pinch of oregano, a clove, stir well, and then put in the birds, turning them in the onion mixture. Cover, and cook slowly on top of the stove for two hours. For the last half hour, cook uncovered and add a little Vermouth as the sauce begins to dry out.

The cooked birds freeze well and can be pulled out of the freezer, resmothered in more melted onions and served for any special guest who may turn up. You may have to pick up the bones in your fingers to get all the delicious bits of meat off them. This is quite permissible, but it is a good idea to have a finger bowl at each place to save your best napkins.

Shad

Last year when the shad were running we were given several beautiful fish from Winyah Bay. A friend who was visiting us, herself a fisherman, had come armed with a scaling knife and another very sharp, long, thin knife. "This is fun," she said, and proceeded to show me how to clean a fish. She worked under running water at the faucet. With the scaling knife she took off all the scales, but was careful not to remove the fins. The reason for this is that many small bones are attached to the fin and when the fish is cooked a yank at the fin will pull them out. Then she cleaned out the gills, just below the head, leaving the head on. With the tip of her long thin knife she cut straight down the narrow line of the belly, exposing the roe. She lifted this out carefully and then removed the rest of the entrails, and washed the fish out carefully. We roasted the shad slowly in a 350° oven. There are various methods of cooking shad in vinegar that completely rid it of bones, but the slow roasting eliminates enough of them without overcooking the fish. You must check and if the oven seems too hot at 350°, reduce it to 300°. The fish should be a beautiful golden-brown when cooked, and the meat should be white and firm. Although the roe can be saved for another day, we cooked it and served it with the fish.

When we first came back to Charleston I was lucky enough to get Helen Brown to tell me how she cooked her marvelous shad roe. Here is the receipt.

Helen Brown's Shad Roe

First, parboil the roe, just covered with water, on low heat for five or six minutes.

Dry it carefully, without breaking the membrane, smear it with bacon grease and a little soft margarine and add a little water to the bottom of the pan so it won't dry out, and cook it covered in a slow oven for at least thirty minutes. Use a covered pan or a pie pan covered with aluminum foil. Just before time to serve it, fry out several strips of bacon, and while it is still limp, before it turns brown, wrap it around the roe and put it under the broiler. Crisp the bacon, one minute is enough, and serve at once.

But test Mrs. Rhett's receipts for yourself! Be brave as Miss Gay was when she made Marie Heyward's Scrapple and reported in some surprise:

"One taste changed our feeling toward it entirely. This is a most delicious dish, one which might well compare with pâté de foie gras as a canapé spread. The flavor is delicate and quite delightful." Of course, but of course.

Elizabeth Verner Hamilton
3 Water Street
February 29, 1976

Pages xiv through 289 of this book were offset from a copy of the first edition (third printing, March 1931) which is in the possession of the South Caroliniana Library of the University of South Carolina, to whose staff the publisher is, for approximately the two-hundredth time,

grateful.

200 YEARS OF
CHARLESTON COOKING

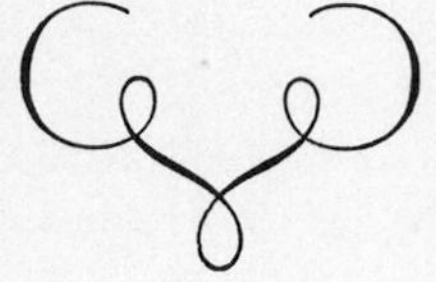

HOW THIS BOOK CAME TO BE

CHARLESTON in South Carolina is a foreign city. In no way does it seem like any other place in America. Just as its fine old houses turn their sides to the street, so does Charleston turn her side and look askance at noise and confusion. Her culture, like her streets, is flower scented. But this is no simple culture. It is the complex outgrowth of a long, slow mixture of peoples, and its natural beauty of blue bay and crystal skies is aglow with rich memories of gracious living. As always in such a civilization, cooking is here not a necessity but an art.

The cooking of Charleston, like the city itself, is like nothing else in the world. It has been my good fortune to keep house for a long time in Paris, and I think that the cooking of Charleston can compare favorably with that of France.

Charleston was settled largely by Huguenots who fled from France and the persecution of Catherine de Medici. These Huguenots have left a deep impression, not only in the architecture and the many French names, but in the kitchen and on the cooking. Later the Negro used her clever mixing spoon in these French recipes, so that what you eat in Charleston today is a slowly ripened mixture of French and Negro cooking.

In the oldest part of the city, where St. Philip's Church lifts its classic spire, the sun casts pointed shadows on a little square. And in that serene spot a small house has dared to have a wild and colorful history of its own. In that little house live ghosts — good, cruel, free-booting ghosts; for here, it is said, Stede Bonnet's pirates used to meet. Over two hundred years ago their meetings came to an end, when they were captured by Colonel William Rhett.

At the side of this old house is a tiny alley along a brick wall. You go down that alley and you are suddenly in an Italian courtyard with grass growing between flags. Before you is a house of old brick and handsome ironwork. This house, a tiny affair, was designed and built by Mrs. Goodwyn (Blanche S.) Rhett, in one of the many crowded moments of her so-called leisure. And one day when I told her that I had no place to lay my head in her lovely city, she said, "I will furnish this for you," which she did in forty-eight hours, with comfort, charm and completeness, from the green and white ice box in the kitchen to the old plantation desk in the living-room. I loved it. It seemed like a playhouse. And there I ate the incredible food prepared by my cook Sally Washington.

When I arrived in Charleston I was ill and rather wobbly. I came to love Charleston better than any place I had ever known in my life. And I wanted to send to a few people for whom I care some of this Charleston. But you cannot send away a place. Places you can describe and photograph, but you cannot share them.

As we sat idly one day in my sunny courtyard, it occurred to me that while places cannot be shared, food you can both describe and share. So I said to Mrs. Rhett, "It's a pity that food like this cannot be eaten in the north. I'd like to send some of these recipes to my friends." She replied with quick enthusiasm, "You write books, why don't you make a book of our recipes? I will get you the recipes from my friends and from my own household." And so she did.

I should like to say here what ought to be said about Mrs. Rhett's lovely house, her talent for hospitality, about the distinguished history of the Rhett family, but Mrs. Rhett will not let me do it. So I cannot.

The gathering of these recipes turned out to be a long job. Most of the old families of the state have special private "receipts" (they use that nice old-fashioned word down there) which are served on special occasions. At state dinners at Mrs. Rhett's, for instance, you will get she-crab soup; at Mr. Edward Hughes', boned turkey with pecan stuffing. These recipes are treasured as closely as is the old sideboard from which dinners have been served for a hundred and fifty years. Not only have they never before been published, but they have never even been given to friends. Such are many of the recipes in this book.

To the housewives of Charleston and their colored cooks, who have contributed the secrets of generations in this book, we are indebted.

There are a few recipes here which appeared a long time ago in *The Carolina Housewife* and *The Southern Cook Book*, little books both out of print for many years. Thumbed, crumpled and rebound copies of them are guarded in a few Charleston kitchens.

But, once gathered, I found that the recipes,

valuable as they were, would never make a book and would never be practical to follow in their original form. So we turned them over to Lettie Gay, director of the New York Herald-Tribune Institute, who has done most of the work of interpreting the " receipts " and has made of this book a professional and not an amateur job.

Thus it turned out that my part consisted, as far as I can see, only in appreciation, or perhaps I should say inspiration, that being the ingredient usually supplied so liberally by the onlooker.

HELEN WOODWARD.

TRIED AND FOUND GOOD

IT'S fun to cook by guess and by golly if you're a good cook to start with; not so much fun if you're inexperienced and eggs are high. A good cook can usually tell at a glance if a recipe will "work" or not, but many a beginner spoils a cake in finding out what was wrong with the directions.

The original recipes in this collection from Charleston were rich in suggestion but poor in precision. To make them more generally useful, each one was tested and standardized in the testing kitchen of the New York Herald-Tribune Institute.

The difficulty in getting a Charleston recipe, we found, is not always due alone to the unwillingness of the cook to part with her secret. Her cooking instinct knows no rules, no measures. She is far more likely to conjure her oven than to use a heat control device. She wouldn't know what to do with a thermometer, but by hunches she knows when to take a boiling syrup off the stove. To translate hunches, a fine mixture of superstitions and a real knowledge of cookery, into intelligible recipes is no easy task, and so it is with no little satisfaction that we offer here a series of authentic Charleston recipes, each one tested and assured.

The object of our testing work was not so much to determine the proper ingredients, for we would trust a Charleston cook to know what seasoning was right, as to be able to report the number of servings. In the days when these recipes were first used families were not only larger than they are now, but there were more servants to feed. We found that in most instances the original recipes could be halved, sometimes cut in thirds, to provide a dish for six persons.

In many recipes it was necessary to make substitutions, as certain ingredients are either no longer available or too expensive for general use. Some recipes, in no wise adaptable to modern use, have been reprinted in their original form simply for the sake of their one-time goodness.

LETTIE GAY

Editor, The New York
Herald-Tribune Institute

SOUPS AND CANAPÉS

In Charleston they still eat dinner at three o'clock in the afternoon. In the days of King George, before the Revolution, elegant people served dinner at three o'clock and Charleston does not like change. By good fortune it is not only the dinner hour which has been preserved; but the secrets of those good things which they ate at their spacious dinners.

As you wake up in the golden mornings in your high ceilinged, paneled room on the Battery overlooking the sea, you do not hear the screech of brakes on a Fifth Avenue Bus. Instead sweet singing slips between the pages of your dreams and you wake to hear a soft negro voice intoning on the streets a song about " She Crab "; he also sells " he " crab, but few buy.

The Crabman charges ten cents a dozen extra for " she " crabs with the eggs in. The crab eggs are picked and put with the crab meat and give a delicious, glutinous quality to the soup which makes it very different from regular crab soup.

"She" Crab Soup belongs especially to the Rhett family and has been served by Mrs. Rhett for presidents and princes. It is prepared always now by Mrs. Rhett's able butler, William Deas, who is one of the great cooks of the world.

It is impossible to get "she" crab except in the laying season; and it is difficult to get it at any time except in places like New York where the markets have everything. But the soup, as tested out in the New York Herald-Tribune Institute, seems to be just as good made with any hard shell crab. Only a little flavor of association would be lost. This soup may, of course, be made with canned crabmeat but the real "she" crab soup as William makes it is worth the extra trouble of picking out the crab-meat.

Crab Soup

1 dozen she crabs
2 cups milk
½ cup cream
1 tablespoon butter
1 small onion
Black pepper and salt
½ teaspoon Worcestershire sauce
1 teaspoon flour
1 tablespoon sherry

Cook the crabs until tender — about twenty minutes in boiling, salted water. Pick the meat from the shells and put the crab meat with the crab eggs into a double boiler. Add the butter, onion and a little black pepper. Let simmer for five minutes. Heat the milk and add to the mixture. Stir together and add the cream and the Worcestershire sauce. Thicken with the flour, add the sherry and salt to taste. Cook over a low flame for one-half hour. Six servings.

— *William's Recipe*

Also from William's skilled hand comes shrimp soup. William never seems to hurry; yet in addition to his elaborate cooking, and in addition to running Mrs. Rhett's elaborate house, William is the leader of a famous quartet which sings spirituals in the old-fashioned way. He has a beautiful tenor voice. Colored people like William seem to accomplish enormous amounts of work without ever being in a hurry and always with time for courtesy.

Once I talked to an old cook down there who did all the work of a large house and then went home and did her own. I said, "Martha, how do you manage to do so much?" And she said, "I never does more than one thing at a time. I does a thing and when it's done I goes on to the next thing."

Shrimp Soup I

2 cups cooked, shelled shrimp
2 tablespoons butter
1 small onion, chopped
$\frac{1}{4}$ teaspoon black pepper
1 quart milk
1 cup cream
Salt
1 tablespoon sherry seasoning

Put the shrimp through the meat grinder. Turn into a double boiler and add the butter, onion and black pepper. Simmer for five minutes, add the milk gradually, stirring constantly, and then add the cream. Salt to taste, using less salt than usual if a salted sherry is to be added. Cook for half an hour, stirring occasionally. Add the sherry just before serving.

This shrimp soup resembles a lobster stew more than anything else we could think of and is a medium thick soup. Without the sherry it would be a fine soup for the children, while the addition of the sherry makes the soup just the thing to serve for a " party " luncheon. The flavor is both delicate and unusual. Six generous servings.

— *William's Recipe*

Shrimp Soup II

First cousin to an oyster stew is the way we would describe this soup:

1 quart milk
1 tablespoon butter
2 teaspoons flour
¼ cup chopped celery
2 cups peeled raw shrimp

Scald the milk, add the butter and flour rubbed together and then the celery. Stir until slightly thickened and add the raw shrimp. Cook gently — we made this soup in a double boiler — for three minutes and season to taste with salt and pepper.

Although the shrimp turn pink in the three minutes specified, they are a bit too gelatinous for our taste. We prefer them well cooked, so we continued the cooking for another ten minutes, stirring occasionally. Serve six.

New Orleans Gumbo

"Take a fowl, cut it up with a piece of fresh beef. Put them in a pot with a little lard, an onion, and water sufficient to cook the meat. After they have become soft, add a hundred oysters with their liquor. Season to your taste and just before taking up the soup, stir in, until it becomes mucilaginous, two spoonfuls of pulverized sassafras leaves."

So goes the old recipe brought long ago to Charleston from New Orleans, and adapted by a generation that ate oysters with epicurean delight. One hundred oysters seem rather many for the average family, so we have reduced the recipe to proportions which yield six plates of delicious gumbo.

1 small chicken
1 pound beef
1 tablespoon lard
1 small onion
3 pints water
2 dozen oysters
1½ teaspoons sassafras leaves or
½ teaspoon file powder
Salt and pepper to taste

In place of the chicken one may use the neck, wings and back of a chicken which is to be used for other purposes and add two or three chicken bouillon cubes. Have the beef cut in small pieces. When the meat is tender and a strong broth has been obtained, cut the chicken in pieces, removing the bones. Add the oysters with their liquor, season to taste with salt and pepper, and add the file powder or sassafras leaves. Cook until the edges of the oysters curl.

Fish Chowder

Wine is added to this chowder; the amount may be varied according to taste.

2 pounds fish
2 large onions
3 slices salt pork
4 sailor's biscuits (pilot biscuit)
Cayenne pepper and spices
2 tablespoons tomato catsup
1 pint wine or cooking sherry

Fry the pork, and in the fat cook the chopped onions. Cut the fish in pieces and wash well. Put the fish into a saucepan with sufficient water to cover. Add the onions and thicken with the pilot biscuits, broken in pieces. Season to taste with Cayenne and spices (nutmeg and allspice are usually used). Cook for about three-quarters of an hour and add the catsup and wine. About an hour is required for the entire cooking.

— *Carolina Housewife*

Turnip Soup

1 pound " scrag of mutton "
1 large onion
1 head of celery
Pepper and salt to taste
2 large turnips

Have a pound of lamb or mutton cut in pieces and add about three pints of water to it. Slice the onion, cut the celery in small pieces and add salt and pepper to taste. Cook these ingredients together until a strong broth is obtained (about an hour or an hour and a half). Meanwhile peel the turnips, cut them in pieces and boil them until tender enough to put through a sieve. Add sufficient turnips to the broth to make it thick (the amount used depends, of course, upon the size of the turnips) and boil the turnips in the broth for about five minutes. Add more salt and pepper if needed and serve very hot. A little cream may, if desired, be added.

Gumbo with Crabs or Shrimp

1 pound beef
½ pound ham
2 tablespoons lard
1 pound peeled shrimp
4 dozen small okra pods
1 large onion
Red pepper and salt

Cut the beef and ham into inch pieces (use ham from the knuckle) and brown them in the hot lard. Add the peeled, raw shrimp and cut in the okra pods and the onion. Season to taste with salt and red pepper. Let all simmer over a slow fire for about twenty minutes; then add enough warm water to cover the contents of the kettle two inches deep. Let this simmer slowly for two hours. If it becomes too thick, more water may be added.

Four large crabs, cut up, may be used in place of the shrimp, or both crabs and shrimp may be added to the gumbo if desired. Chicken may be substituted for the beef for a more delicate soup.

—*Southern Cook Book*

Calf's Head Soup

It was impossible to test this soup in New York, but we give the recipe as it was written for the benefit of readers who can obtain this most necessary ingredient.

Boil the head in three quarts of water until tender; then cut it up and take out bones. Season with allspice, cloves, mace, curry powder, salt, pepper, parsley and onions. Take brains, and stir up with an egg and a little flour and thicken the soup when almost done.

—*Charlotte Ball* (*An old recipe from the Bluff Plantation, Cooper River*)

Chicken Custard

While this delicately flavored custard could be served either hot or cold, we think it would be especially attractive served in green custard cups, very thoroughly chilled, as the beginning of a summer luncheon.

1 cup strong chicken broth
1 cup thin cream
3 egg yolks
Salt to taste

Scald together the chicken broth and cream. (If a thicker custard is preferred, use heavy cream.) Pour the scalded mixture over the well beaten egg yolks, and cook in a double boiler, stirring constantly, until slightly thickened. Salt to taste and serve in custard cups.

Oyster Soup

1 pint oysters (2 dozen)
4 cups liquor from oysters
1 tablespoon butter
1 cup cream
$\frac{1}{8}$ teaspoon nutmeg
$\frac{1}{8}$ teaspoon mace
Pepper and salt to taste
Flour if necessary

Remove the oysters from their liquor and bring the liquor to the boiling point. Skim it and add the water, butter, cream and seasonings. Bring again to the boiling point and, just before serving, add the oysters. Cook until the edges of the oysters curl, and serve. If the soup seems too thin, add a tablespoon or two of flour mixed to a thin paste with cold milk and cook until the mixture thickens slightly. This will serve four. The nutmeg and mace give an unusual flavor which appears to be a Charleston favorite.

—*Mrs. William A. Hutchinson*

Egg Soup

This is an old German recipe taken from the *Carolina Housewife*, a little old book, long out of print, of which a few copies are guarded like jewels by Charleston ladies. The last of it reads, "If the bouillon be of chicken, you may put it back into the bouillon; you may also add asparagus and green peas, both being already boiled." The time of year when we tested this recipe prevented our having the fresh vegetables on hand, but they would undoubtedly be a delicious addition.

4 eggs
$\frac{1}{8}$ teaspoon nutmeg
1 tablespoon chopped parsley
4 ounces bread crumbs
2 quarts bouillon

Beat the eggs, add the nutmeg, parsley and bread crumbs and mix well together. Add the bouillon carefully, stirring constantly, and cook for ten minutes, stirring almost continually. If bouillon cubes are used, no salt will be required, otherwise, add salt to taste. This will serve eight.

— *Carolina Housewife*

Oyster Stew with Mace

The most important social event of the year in Charleston is the St. Cecelia Ball. The society which holds this function was organized in 1737 to give concerts, for as early as this Charleston expressed an æsthetic tendency. Each year since 1822 the Society has given a stately ball, whose ritual is formal even in these days of freedom. Mrs. St. Julien Ravenel says in her interesting book on Charleston: "Only in the sixties, as during the Revolution, all the men being in the field, and the city under fire, the ball was necessarily interrupted.

"The Society elects its members; names must be offered at the annual meeting by a letter presented by a member. If a man's father or grandfather, or any of his immediate kindred, have belonged before him, there is little doubt that he will be chosen. Nevertheless blackballs (two suffice to exclude) have fallen, when the applicant was a notoriously unworthy scion of his family tree. If a new resident, or a family recently brought into notice, there will be inquiry, perhaps hesitation, and a good backing will be desirable. But if he be of a character and standing calculated to make his membership acceptable to the society, he will be elected — unless he has some adversary; then he may fail. The presenter of such a one will make careful examination into public feeling before subjecting his friend to mortification, and will withhold the letter if in doubt. When a man is elected, the names of the ladies of his household are at once put upon 'the list' and remain there forever. Only death or removal from the city erases them, — change of fortune affects them not at all. To be dropped from the St. Cecelia is an awful possibility sometimes hinted at, but which (as far as known) has never come to pass."

Pity the Charleston girl of social aspirations who cannot go to the St. Cecelia Ball.

One of the special Charleston dishes often served at the St. Cecelia Ball is oyster soup with mace.

1 quart oysters
1 cup water
1 tablespoon butter
1 tablespoon flour
2 cups cream
Salt and pepper to taste
2 blades mace

Scald the oysters in their own liquor. As soon as they are plump remove them to another dish. Add to the liquor the water and the butter and flour mixed together well. Then pour in the cream, season to taste with salt and pepper and add the mace. Let this become very hot; then add the oysters. As soon as the oysters are heated remove the mace from the stew and serve. This makes eight plates of soup.

— *Alicia Rhett Mayberry*

Appetizer

Rounds of whole wheat bread
Butter
1 cream cheese
3 tablespoons mayonnaise
1 can skinless and boneless sardines
1 hard cooked egg
2 tablespoons chopped celery
2 teaspoons Worcestershire sauce
½ teaspoon tabasco sauce
½ teaspoon salt
6 very small tomatoes
Mayonnaise
Pimientos
Shredded lettuce

Sauté the rounds of bread in the butter and spread them with the cream cheese mixed with three tablespoons of mayonnaise. Mash the sardines, add the chopped egg, celery and the seasonings. Mix well with mayonnaise and fill the tomatoes, which should be hollowed out, rubbed with salt and allowed to drain and chill for at least two hours before they are used. Place the filled tomatoes on the toast rounds and garnish with pimentos and shredded lettuce.

— *Mrs. Richardson, Columbia, South Carolina*

Cheese Canapés

These are excellent to serve with cocktails.

Small rounds of toast
1 cup cream cheese
1 teaspoon onion juice
½ teaspoon tabasco sauce

Mix the cheese with the seasonings, adding cream to moisten if necessary, and spread on the toast.

— *Mrs. Richardson, Columbia, South Carolina*

Cocktail Sauce for Shrimp

1 cup mayonaise
2 tablespoons catsup
2 tablespoons chili sauce
1 tablespoon taragon vinegar
1 teaspoon lemon juice

Combine the ingredients and turn over chilled shrimp. Sufficient for eight cocktails. Allow six shrimp for each cocktail unless a very heavy dinner is following, in which case three or four will be enough.

—*Mrs. William A. Hutchinson*

This sauce was pronounced "the best I've ever tasted" by every one we know who has eaten it.

SHELLFISH AND FISH

CHARLESTON sits down in its marshes by the sea, the old dreaming city. Lazy rivers slip by on each side, and along their banks sleep silent old plantation houses. Everywhere you look there is water. Between the city and the sea lie strips of small islands with white, wide, sandy beaches. All these waters are rich in fish, so that each morning from island and bay and river come negroes bearing baskets — the shrimp man and the crab man, the fish man and the oyster man, each singing a song about his wares.

Mrs. Kate Hagood Tobin listened and wrote down the words of the shrimp man's song:

Oh, lady, if yo' want to see somethin' fine,
Jes' look in dis li'l green cyaht ob mine,
An' you will see de tender, pure raw s'rimp.

Another verse ran:

Oh, lady, if yo' want to tas'e somethin' sweet,
Jes' take a li'l onion an' a li'l piece o' meat
An' mix 'em wid yo' tender, pure, raw s'rimp.

Mrs. Tobin says she tried the following recipe and found it good.

Green Corn Pie with Shrimp I

2 cups corn
2 eggs, beaten slightly
1 tablespoon butter, melted
½ cup milk
1 cup peeled raw shrimp
Salt and pepper to taste

Grate enough corn to make two cups, or, if canned corn is used, have it well drained. Add the eggs, melted butter, milk, shrimp and seasonings. Turn into a casserole and bake in a slow oven (300 degrees F.) for about half an hour. This recipe may be varied by substituting tomato juice for the milk. Serves six. A similar dish, but one that is much less rich, follows.

As any good cook book will tell you, shrimp can be peeled either before or after cooking but they are pleasanter to handle after they have been cooked from three to five minutes — just long enough to make them turn pink.

Green Corn Pie with Shrimp II

Several ears of corn or two cans of corn
1 egg, beaten

1 tablespoon butter
1 cup milk
1 cup shrimp
Salt and pepper to taste

Grate enough corn to make two cupfuls of mush (if canned corn is used, drain off liquid). Add beaten egg, butter, milk, salt, pepper and raw shrimp. If preferred, use the liquor from the canned corn instead of milk and add one-half cup of tomato juice. Put into deep dish and bake one-half hour.

This recipe is also delicious without shrimp.

—*Miss Ethel Norvell*

Shrimp Patties

1 cup cooked, shelled shrimp
2 slices bread, cut one inch thick
1 tablespoon butter
$\frac{1}{4}$ teaspoon mace
$\frac{1}{4}$ teaspoon black pepper
Salt to taste

The shrimp should be pounded in a mortar, according to the original directions, but we found that running them through a meat grinder gave satisfactory results with much less work. Cut the crusts off the bread, which should be rather stale. Turn water over it, squeeze dry, and crumble into the shrimp. Add the butter and seasonings and mix well. Shape into little cakes and bake in a buttered pan in a moderate oven until brown, or sauté in butter, turning to brown both sides.

These shrimp patties would be a delicious entrée to serve at a luncheon. Served with a sauce, bland so that it will not mask the delicate shrimp flavor, they would be excellent as a course of a formal dinner.

Shrimps with Hominy

This is a delicious breakfast dish, served in almost every house in Charleston during the shrimp season.

1 pound raw shrimp
½ cup butter
Salt and black pepper
2 cups cooked hominy

Shell the shrimp, put them into a saucepan in which the butter has been melted, add the seasonings and stir until the shrimp are hot. They may then be covered, stirred occasionally, and allowed to cook for ten minutes. Serve with the hot hominy. This will make four servings.

A charming old gentleman seventy-eight years old avers that as far back as he could remember he has eaten shrimp with hominy for breakfast every morning during the shrimp season, and shrimp salad for supper every Sunday night, and he has never tired of it.

— *William's Recipe*

Shrimp Pie I

2 cups peeled, cooked shrimp
3 slices bread, cut ½ inch thick
1 cup milk
2 tablespoons butter, melted
½ teaspoon black pepper
1 teaspoon Worcestershire sauce
2 tablespoons sherry seasoning
Mace and nutmeg to taste

Soak the bread in the milk and mash with a fork. Add the shrimp, butter and seasonings. Turn into a buttered casserole and bake in a moderately hot oven (375 degrees F.) for twenty minutes.

This dish would be particularly good as a Sunday night supper main course served with a green salad. Six servings.

Shrimp Pie II

A heartier concoction, this, than the first shrimp pie, and more suited for a week-day, one-dish meal than its predecessor.

2 cups peeled shrimp
4 slices stale bread
1 No. 2 can tomatoes
1 green pepper, chopped fine
1 tablespoon butter
1 small onion, chopped
2 or 3 hard-cooked eggs
Salt and pepper to taste

Fry the onion gently in the butter until brown. Break up the bread in little pieces and mix with the tomatoes. Then add to the butter and onion with the pepper, shrimp and seasonings and cook for about twenty minutes. Add the chopped eggs and turn into a shallow baking dish. Sprinkle with toasted bread crumbs and dot with bits of butter. Bake in a moderate oven for about fifteen minutes.

It chanced that when we first tested this recipe our only stale bread was whole wheat. The combination was such a good one that we consider ourselves fortunate to have happened upon it. Six servings. —*Mrs. Pinckney*

Shrimp Pie III

1 pound cooked, shelled shrimp
2 slices bread cut $1\frac{1}{2}$ inches thick
1 cup wine (sherry flavoring)
2 tablespoons butter
Salt, pepper, nutmeg and mace to taste

Cut the crust from the bread and mash the crumbs to a paste with the wine and butter. A fork is the best tool to use for this process. Season to taste with salt, pepper, nutmeg and mace and add the shrimp. Turn into a buttered baking dish and bake in a moderate oven (350 degrees F.) about forty-five minutes. The dish has a strong wine flavor. It will serve six.

In making this recipe, we used the shrimp broken in pieces. If they were ground before adding them to the bread crumbs, the texture would be more even and we rather think that the flavor of the shrimp would be more pronounced.

Oysters or crabmeat may be substituted for the shrimp in making this recipe.

Shrimp Pie IV

Although this shrimp pie has the nutmeg to be found in most recipes, it uses milk in place of wine for moistening the bread.

1 pound shrimp
2 large slices bread
1 cup milk, scalded
1 tablespoon butter
Red pepper, nutmeg and salt

Boil the shrimp for about five minutes, shell them, and leave them whole or grind them as you prefer. The ground shrimp give a more uniform texture to the dish and a more decidedly shrimp flavor. Soak the bread in the scalded milk and mash it with a fork. Add the butter, seasonings to taste and the shrimp. Turn into a buttered baking dish and bake in a moderate oven (350 degrees F.) for half an hour.

—*Martha Laurens Patterson*

Shrimp Pilau

4 slices bacon
1 small onion
2½ cups canned tomatoes
1 cup rice (uncooked)
1½ cups peeled cooked shrimp
Salt to taste

Cut the bacon into inch pieces and fry until crisp. Remove from the pan and brown the onion, chopped fine, in the bacon fat. Add the tomatoes and let cook for a few minutes. Then add the rice and steam in the upper part of a double boiler until the rice is cooked—about forty-five minutes. Add the shrimp and bacon and turn into a baking dish. Bake in a moderate oven for about fifteen minutes. This should be rather solid in texture, and the rice, while perfectly cooked, will not be as soft as when cooked by our usual method of boiling in quantities of water. Serves six.

Green Corn and Shrimp Pudding

6 large ears of corn
3 eggs, separated
2 teaspoons sugar
1 tablespoon melted butter
½ teaspoon salt
2 pounds shrimp, cooked and shelled

Grate the corn from the cob. Beat the whites and yolks of the eggs separately. Add the egg yolks to the corn and beat well. Then add the butter, the milk gradually, beating all the while, and then the sugar, salt and the shrimp. Lastly, fold in the egg whites stiffly beaten. Turn into a buttered casserole and bake in a slow oven (300 degrees F.) about an hour, removing the cover at the last so that the dish will brown. This will serve from six to eight.

—*Mrs. E. H. Sparkman*

Baked Shrimps and Tomatoes

2 pounds shrimp
1 rule baking-powder biscuit dough
2 tablespoons butter
Pepper, mace or nutmeg, and salt
2 cups stewed tomatoes

Boil the shrimp for a few minutes until they turn pink and remove the shells. Butter a deep dish well, and put in it a layer of baking-powder biscuit dough (pounded biscuit is used for the real southern dish, but few of us have time to make beaten biscuit now, alas!). On the dough put a layer of shrimp with small pieces of butter, pepper, salt and mace or nutmeg sprinkled over them. Then add a layer of stewed tomatoes with more of the butter, pepper and salt and cover with a very thin layer of biscuit dough. Add another layer of shrimp and continue until all the ingredients are used, making the top layer of biscuit. Bake in a hot oven (425 degrees F.) for about forty-five minutes and serve piping hot. Serves eight.

—*Carolina Housewife*

Shrimp Paste I

From all over the world visitors come to see Magnolia Gardens, now owned by C. Norwood Hastie. Sometimes two thousand people a day drive up along the moss-hung roads to see the acres of azaleas that blaze here in the spring. Everyone who has walked in these paths of flowered magnificence will feel a special pleasure in using this recipe, one which the owners of Magnolia have used for generations. Mrs. Hastie's shrimp paste is very different from the other recipes for this delicacy. It is highly seasoned by the peppers and would be excellent as a part of a cold meat plate. The paste might also be served as a cold entrée.

2 pounds shrimp
2 green peppers
1 small red onion
1 tablespoon Worcestershire sauce
½ teaspoon French mustard
1 teaspoon vinegar
Red pepper

Boil the shrimp, remove the shells and put the fish through the meat grinder. Also grind up the green peppers and red onion and mix these ingredients well together. Then add the Worcestershire sauce, mustard, vinegar and red pepper to taste.

Make a thick white sauce consisting of:

3 tablespoons butter
⅓ cup flour
1 cup milk
¼ teaspoon salt

Add this to the shrimp mixture. Put in individual molds and press down firmly with a spoon. When thoroughly cold, unmold. This serves eight.

— *Mrs. C. Norwood Hastie*

Shrimp Paste II

The possibilities for this delightfully flavored shrimp butter are many. The shrimp taste is pronounced, yet it combines with the butter to make a dish which can only be described as "delicate." We suggest serving a slice of the shrimp paste as part of an *hors-d'oeuvres,* or as a slice on a cold meat plate; also use the paste to stuff celery or as a sandwich filling.

½ cup butter
1 pound cooked, shelled shrimp
Salt to taste

Cream the butter until very soft. Grind the shrimp fine by putting them through the meat chopper, and mix with the butter, creaming the mixture well. Salt to taste and pack in an oblong dish. Bake in a moderate oven (350 degrees F.) for thirty minutes or until it leaves the sides of the dish and is a trifle brown on top. Allow to cool. Put in the refrigerator overnight before slicing.

—*Miss Loulie Porcher*

Shrimp Paste III

1 pound shrimp, cooked and peeled
½ pound butter
½ teaspoon salt

$\frac{1}{8}$ teaspoon celery salt
$\frac{1}{8}$ teaspoon Cayenne pepper
$\frac{1}{2}$ teaspoon nutmeg
Toast crumbs

Grind the shrimp very fine. Cream the butter until soft and add the ground shrimp, mixing well. Then add the seasonings and combine thoroughly. Place in an oblong baking dish and sprinkle toast crumbs over the top of the shrimp mixture. Brown in a hot oven (400 degrees F.) for about three minutes. Cool and place in the refrigerator until time to serve (for several hours at least).

This paste is not as firm as the preceding one, and it has a much more buttery flavor. The nutmeg is quite noticeable, although it blends well with the shrimp.

—*Mrs. Walter Pringle*

Fish Soufflé

1 pound coarse fish
(rock fish, haddock, or cod)
6 egg whites
Salt and pepper

Whip the egg whites stiffly and add the flaked fish. Beat together until stiff again and season to taste with salt and pepper. Turn into a buttered casserole and bake in a moderate oven (325 degrees F.) for about forty-five minutes. Serve at once with what is called in the South brown butter, in the North lemon butter. This amount makes eight servings.

—*William's Recipe*

Devilled Crabs

One dozen fresh crabs are required for this recipe, but it may also be made using canned crabmeat and baked in a casserole instead of in the crab shells.

2 cups crabmeat
¼ teaspoon mustard
¼ teaspoon nutmeg
¼ teaspoon mace
2 cloves
1 tablespoon melted butter
1 egg, separated
Salt and pepper
½ cup wine or sherry flavoring
Cracker crumbs

Add the seasonings to the crabmeat, stir in the melted butter and the beaten egg yolk. Add the cooking sherry and season to taste with salt and pepper. Fold in the stiffly beaten egg white. Fill the crab-backs or put into a buttered baking dish, sprinkle with cracker crumbs and bake in a moderate oven (350 degrees F.) for half an hour.

—*Mrs. E. H. Sparkman*

Baked Shad

1 large shad
2 cups fine bread crumbs
1 onion, chopped fine
1 tablespoon parsley, chopped
Salt and pepper
¼ cup butter, melted

Select a large shad and have the head cut off and the fish cleaned without slitting it (it must not be cut open since it is to be stuffed). For the stuffing, mix the chopped onion and parsley with the bread crumbs, season to taste with salt and pepper and moisten with the melted butter. The dressing should be rather dry, but a few drops of water may be needed to moisten it.

Stuff the fish, put it into a baking pan, season with salt and pepper and sprinkle bread crumbs over it. Dot the fish with lumps of butter, turn some water into the pan, sprinkle a tablespoon or two of flour over it, put the pan into a moderately hot oven (375 degrees F.) and bake it for one and a half hours. While baking, it must be basted occasionally with the gravy to prevent its becoming too dry.

—*Carolina Housewife*

Tomato Sauce for Baked Fish

You cannot, outside of South Carolina, get drum roe from Beaufort. You cannot get Folly Island clams, or stone crab, or the Edisto River Brim of unforgettable flavor. But you can take any kind of baked fish and trim it with this tomato sauce. Fillets of haddock baked and served with this sauce are excellent.

¼ cup cooking oil
2 large onions, sliced
2 tablespoons flour
1 No. 2 can tomatoes
½ cup sherry flavoring
Cayenne pepper, cloves and thyme

Heat the oil in a saucepan and add the onions. Cook until tender and golden brown. Then stir in the flour and add the tomatoes strained through a sieve. Bring to the boiling point, stirring constantly, and add the cooking sherry. Season to taste with Cayenne pepper, a few cloves and a little thyme if desired. Let simmer gently for about three minutes and pour over the baked fish.

Pine Bark Stew

This stew has been used for many years at Otranto Club. Here is the recipe as given to Theodore J. Simons by Captain John A. Kelley of Kingstree, South Carolina.

The stew is best made in the open, in the old-fashioned deep Dutch oven that will hold three or four gallons. The fire should be made ahead of time so as to insure a large quantity of coals giving a steady, slow heat.

For a party of thirty: Slice 1 pound of strip bacon. Try out all the grease possible and fry about four sliced onions in this fat. Then add hot water for about two inches in the receptacle. Place a layer of fish on top of this, then a layer of sliced Irish potatoes and sliced onions, a layer of fish and a layer of potatoes and so on until the quantity required has been put in the receptacle. While it is boiling see that there is put in a liberal supply of salt and about one tablespoon of curry powder. This should stew slowly for about three-quarters of an hour. The fish, potatoes and onions should be entirely covered with water. While it is boiling have on the fire nearby a good-sized saucepan with one pound of melted butter. When this is thoroughly melted and hot, add to it gradually the boiling stew and flavor with the following:

One small bottle of Worcestershire sauce, one large bottle of tomato catsup, teaspoonful of red pepper, liberal supply of black pepper, 1 tablespoon curry powder. Stir the sauce frequently, keep it on a slow heat, and continue to dip from the fish stew into the sauce until it cooks thoroughly. The color will become like that of chocolate or pine bark, and because of this, perhaps, some wag on the Pee Dee gave it its name no one knows how long ago. Another explanation of the name is that it was taken from the pine bark used to start the fires on the river bank. This stew should be served on toast with rice and an abundance of gravy poured over the fish. The preference is for redbreast (sunfish), blue bream, or bass in steaks. For salt-water fish, use small sheepshead. It requires a firm boiling fish and the object is to serve the fish whole with a liberal supply of gravy.

Fried Fish

In all stories about negroes is the sizzling sound of frying fish, the inviting smell and the delicious taste; but that delicious taste does not have to be restricted to fiction. You can have it in your own dining-room by following their very simple method of frying fish.

Roll the fish in corn meal, fry it in deep bacon fat, cooking fat or butter and dry (drain) it thoroughly before serving — that is all there is to it.

Sheepshead (a Favorite Charleston Fish)

1 large sheepshead fish
Salt
Juice of 1 lemon
1 small can tomatoes
1 tablespoon butter
1 tablespoon flour
1 teaspoon onion juice
1 teaspoon salt
Pepper to taste

Boil the sheepshead until tender; salt and sprinkle it with the lemon juice. Serve with a sauce made by adding the butter and flour mixed together to the scalded tomatoes. Add the seasonings and cook until slightly thickened.

— *Mrs. Rhett*

Stuffed Crabs and Mushrooms

2 tablespoons butter
1 tablespoon flour
½ cup cream
1 cup mushrooms
1 pound cooked crabmeat
Juice of ½ lemon
1 teaspoon capers
1 teaspoon chopped parsley
2 egg whites, beaten stiff

Melt the butter and add the mushrooms, sliced or chopped. Cook until they are tender. Remove the mushrooms or put them to one side of the pan and add the flour. When that is well blended add the cream. When the cream sauce is thick, remove from the fire and add the other ingredients in the order given. Put the mixture back into the crab shells, or if the shells are not available (this dish is delicious made from canned crabmeat!), bake in a buttered casserole in a moderate oven (350 degrees F.) for about twenty minutes. Eight servings.

— *William's Recipe*

Oysters à la Newburg

3 dozen oysters
1 cup heavy cream
1 tablespoon butter
2 tablespoons flour
Yolks of 3 hard-cooked eggs
½ cup sherry flavoring
Cayenne pepper and salt to taste

Cook the oysters in their liquor until the edges curl, then drain off the liquor. Heat the cream very hot and add the flour and butter creamed together and the hard-cooked egg yolks, mashed fine. Cook together until thick and then add the sherry. Season with Cayenne and salt (little if any salt will be needed if a salted sherry has been used) and mix with the oysters. Put into a shallow baking dish, cover with buttered crumbs, if desired, and bake in a moderately hot oven (375 degrees F.) for about twenty minutes. This very rich dish will serve six.

Oysters In Bread Cases

24 oysters
2 tablespoons butter
2 tablespoons flour
⅛ teaspoon mace
⅛ teaspoon thyme
1 teaspoon chopped parsley
2 anchovies
6 rolls
Butter
1 cup cream
1 egg yolk
2 teaspoons lemon juice

Cook the oysters in their own liquor until the edges curl. Remove them and to the liquor add the butter and flour well blended, the mace, thyme, parsley and the anchovies. Let it simmer gently for about five minutes. Remove the crumb from the rolls, leaving cases which should be sautéed in butter until a little brown on each side. Add the cream to the oyster liquor, return the oysters to it and add the beaten egg yolk, being careful that the mixture does not curdle. Cook for a minute or two more and add the lemon juice. Serve at once. This is sufficient for six servings and makes an excellent luncheon dish or entrée.

Terrapin

None of the terrapin dishes could be tested. The following recipes are given as they were originally recorded.

Terrapin Soup

1 large fresh-water terrapin
2 quarts water
1 slice bacon
2 dozen cloves
5 dozen allspice
Salt, red and black pepper
Browned flour
½ cup wine or sherry flavoring
½ nutmeg, grated

Clean the terrapin and put it into a large kettle. Add the water, bacon, cloves, allspice, salt and pepper and boil slowly for three or four hours. Then thicken it with browned flour. Just before serving, add the wine in which has been grated the nutmeg.

—*Carolina Housewife*

Cooter (Terrapin) Stew

"Cooters," fresh-water terrapin, are comparatively little used in the North, but Charleston has several famous recipes which call for them. The directions for a cooter stew which will serve twelve people are as follows:

Cut off the heads of four cooters. Cut off the shells with a hatchet or sharp knife. Take out the meat and eggs (if any) and scald the feet to get the skin off. Put all except the eggs in a pot of warm water and stew with salt until tender. Take out and remove all the large bones. Return to the pot and season with the following:

1 teaspoon allspice
1 blade mace
12 cloves
A little red pepper

When nearly done, thicken with brown flour. Let all cook slowly for several hours. Just before serving put in a wine glass of sherry and drop in the eggs. Cut up a lemon very fine and put into the serving dish. Pour the stew over it and serve.

—*Fannie Ferguson Heyward,*
Dockon Plantation, Cooper River

Calabash (Terrapin in the Back)

The rice field " cooter " or terrapin is first killed and allowed to drip, head down. In extracting the meat remove the bottom of the shell. Care should be taken to get this out in as large pieces as possible. This should then be boiled for at least four to five hours over a slow heat, depending upon age of the terrapin, when a rich brown thick soup or stew is obtained. Seasoning should be added at time of boiling, such as salt, pepper (red and black). Some prefer a small quantity of white or Irish potatoes and a little onion. When thoroughly cooked, the meat should be cut into small pieces with a sharp knife or scissors, *across grain*, for if cut otherwise, it will have a tendency to become stringy.

The back of the " cooter," having been cleaned thoroughly both inside and out, is then used as the container for the stew, to which is added bread or biscuit crumbs and ample butter. This is placed in the upper part of the oven, a slow heat rather than a fast one being preferable, for about one-half hour, after which time the top will form a brown and crispy crust. Particular care should be exercised to serve very hot.

This is a recipe which you may never use unless you have a most elaborate household and live in a neighborhood where terrapin is common. It is included here partly because of its historical interest. Of Indian origin, refined by three hundred years of use in white households, it is rarely cooked now, perhaps once every five or ten years, when a most distinguished guest comes to South Carolina. The art of cooking calabash is preserved by a few Negroes, mostly very old. The recipe here given was obtained from Joe Robertson, an old colored man from the country, servant of Mr. Robert Harleston of Bossis Plantation, whose great dinners have slipped into history, but whose recipes appear from time to time in this book.

Calabash II

Prepare the terrapin as for soup, put it on to boil with just enough water to cover it (long boiling makes it stringy), season with black and red pepper, salt, onion and a little thyme. When the flesh becomes tender, remove all bones and thicken with wheat flour or cornstarch which has been mixed with cold water to the consistency of cream, and is free from lumps. Let the terrapin boil long enough to cook the flour. Remove from the fire and add one good tablespoon of butter, a wine glass of wine or good whiskey, a pinch of cloves and mace to the taste and lemon to the taste. Have the back of the terrapin ready, which must be scalded and scraped, make a stiff dough of flour and water, form a bank around the shell, pour the mixture in and dust the top over well with pounded biscuit crumbs. Lay several terrapin eggs, which have been boiled and removed from the shell, over the top, and heat in the oven until the top is of a light brown.

—Caroline P. Rutledge,
Hampton Plantation, Santee River

PILAUS, EGG DISHES AND OTHER MAIN DISHES

The Oxford Dictionary says that a pilau is an Oriental dish of rice with meat and spices. Yet few foods seem to be so at home in South Carolina as pilaus. Doubtless the early traders brought the idea of pilaus from India in the days when Charleston was a great seaport, before the Revolutionary War. And the southern cooks shifted the emphasis from the second to the first syllable, and the ingredients from oil to tomatoes. For down in Charleston they pronounce it pélos, and they cook it so that the dish comes out dry and greaseless. In the North these recipes will be a godsend to those who have left-overs. But in the South you never have such a thing. A pilau is a dish of amazing variations. It can be rich or parsimonious, as you will. Rice is its main ingredient, which is only fitting in a country where so much rice was grown.

Until twenty-five years ago the low country around Charleston grew fat and rich on rice.

Rice plantations extended through the marshes to the sea and their owners traveled luxuriously in Europe or lived in state in fine houses along the Battery of Charleston. Then Texas came along with cheaper methods of growing rice, and the rice plantations went back to futile, lovely and silent marsh.

It was by a romantic accident that rice was first successfully grown in South Carolina. In 1694 a vessel set out from Madagascar, then as remote in the thought of America as Mars might seem today. She was bound for Liverpool but was blown so far off her course that she put into Charleston for repairs. Landgrave Thomas Smith boarded the ship, whether for duty or pleasure it is not stated. The captain presented him with a small package of rough rice for seed. The Landgrave planted it in the proper marshy soil and there sprang up a crop so large that he was able to supply the whole colony. Thus from a storm-tossed ship grew the enormous rice wealth of South Carolina.

The squab pilau given here is the one used by Mrs. Rhett for formal occasions. You can judge for yourself from this list of ingredients that squab pilau is a dish for your most special dinner guests.

Roast Squab with Rice Pilau

4 squabs
6 slices bacon
1 onion
$\frac{3}{4}$ cup chopped celery
2 cups rice
4 cups chicken stock
4 eggs
Salt and pepper
Mustard pickle juice

Dress the squabs as usual. For the stuffing use a rice pilau made as follows: Dice the bacon and cook until crisp. Remove the bacon and add the chopped celery and onion to the bacon drippings and let them brown. Cook the rice in the chicken stock until tender and add the bacon and onion and celery mixture. Beat the eggs and add to the rice, stirring well so that the heat of the rice may cook the eggs, and season to taste with salt and pepper. Stuff the squabs with the mixture and make mounds of the remainder on which to lay the squabs. Bake in a hot oven (425 degrees F.) for about twenty-five minutes, basting the squabs frequently with mustard pickle juice. The mustard pickle adds a piquancy to the squabs and combines well with the pilau stuffing.

—*Mrs. Rhett*

Okra Pilau I

My cook in Charleston was called Washington. Her full name was Sally Washington, but naturally no one ever called her Sally. She was in the traditional manner, or as one might say, old-fashioned. She was one of those round jolly looking Negroes, round-eyed, round-bodied and round in disposition. As she worked she sang spirituals softly to herself all day long. She and her three daughters had enough energy and character to supply several families.

Her cooking was of a kind to make one speculate as to whether she was a genius in her own right or whether Charleston was gifted by the gods. Her cooking was simple. It was not suited to great functions. Her okra pilau, for instance, given below, was so simple that it can be prepared in any household.

3 slices bacon, cut in dice
1 cup rice
1 cup okra
2 cups water

Brown the bacon, and remove it from the fat. Cut the okra in small pieces and fry in the bacon drippings until it stops stringing. The fire should be low during this process, since over too hot a flame the okra burns very easily. Add the rice and cold water, cover and let steam until done (about forty minutes). Add the bacon dice and serve. This will serve four.

— *Washington's Recipe*

Okra Pilau II

For a more elaborate okra pilau we leave Charleston and go to the up-country. In Columbia, the capital of the state, Mrs. Richardson is a famous hostess. You are expected to compliment her on her cookery and you do with simple-hearted enthusiasm.

4 slices bacon
1 onion, chopped
2 cups stewed tomatoes
1 tablespoon green pepper
2 cups okra, sliced thin
Salt and black pepper
2 quarts water
2 cups rice
1 teaspoon salt

Dice the bacon and cook in a deep frying pan until golden brown. Lift out the bacon and fry the onion and minced green pepper in the bacon fat until brown. Then add the tomatoes and okra (measured after slicing) and let them cook down, stirring occasionally to prevent burning. Season well with salt and pepper.

Meanwhile cook the rice in the two quarts of water, to which a teaspoon of salt has been added. After the rice has boiled for twelve minutes drain, mix with the tomato mixture and turn into the top of a double boiler. Let it steam for fifteen or twenty minutes, at the end of which time the rice should be tender and thoroughly flavored with the tomato. Add the bacon before serving. If it is added too far ahead of time it will lose its crispness. This will serve six generously.

— *Mrs. Richardson*

Carolina Tomato Pilau

Make exactly the same as the okra pilau, eliminating the okra.

Tomato Pilau

5 small slices salt pork, diced
1 small onion, chopped
1 No. 2 can tomatoes
2 cups cooked rice
½ cup water
Salt to taste
3 tablespoons butter

Fry the diced salt pork in a saucepan with the onion until brown. Add the tomatoes and cook over a slow fire for ten minutes, then add the water and salt to taste. Stir in the rice and let the pilau cook slowly until all the liquid is absorbed. Just before serving, stir in the butter.

— *William's Recipe*

Egg Pilau

From Columbia also comes Mrs. Salley's egg pilau, a truly marvelous concoction for Sunday night supper.

2 cups rice
2 teaspoons salt
4 cups chicken stock
½ cup butter
6 eggs
Pepper to taste

Cook the rice with the salt in the chicken stock, keeping the kettle tightly covered during the cooking process. The rice will absorb all the stock and should be done in about twenty minutes. As soon as it is done stir in the eggs (they may be broken into another dish and all added at once) and beat for a minute or two, adding the butter at this time. The heat of the rice will cook the eggs and melt the butter without returning the pan to the fire. Season to taste with black pepper and serve at once.

This will serve eight and furnishes a creamy rice dish which suggests scrambled eggs and has a decided chicken flavor.

— *Mrs. I. E. Salley*

Chicken Pilau I

A really marvelous pilau is made with chicken.

6 tablespoons butter
6 stalks celery, cut up
1 onion, chopped
2 tomatoes, sliced
2 cups rice
1 chicken (2½ pounds), cut as for frying
Chicken broth
Salt and pepper

Brown onion, celery and tomatoes separately in butter. Put the raw rice into a saucepan, cover with the browned celery, onion and tomatoes and the raw chicken. Pour over this enough chicken broth to cover (chicken bouillon cubes or canned soup may be used). Cover with a tightly fitting lid and cook slowly for one-half hour. If a larger chicken is used it should be boiled first until half tender and the broth then used on the rice. This recipe serves six.

Chicken Pilau II

1 fat hen
2 cups uncooked rice
2 green peppers
Salt to taste
¼ cup butter

Boil the hen until it is tender. Add the rice to the water left in the pot — there should be about a quart — and put in the peppers, cut up, and salt to taste. Cover and cook until the rice is soft. Then add the butter and the chicken cut in pieces, and serve.

— *Essie Woodward Messervy*

Chicken Pilau III

2 cups uncooked rice
5 cups boiling water
2 teaspoons salt
1 chicken
$\frac{1}{4}$ pound salt pork
1 large onion, finely minced
Pepper to taste

Cook the rice in the five cups of boiling water to which the salt has been added. Keep the saucepan closely covered during the cooking. The rice should be dry when done. Parboil the chicken and the white pork till very tender. Remove the chicken from the stock, add the onion and season with pepper. Cook the stock down for a few minutes until the onion is tender. Take the chicken from the bones and mix with the rice, adding sufficient stock to flavor. Do not add too much of the stock, as the dish should be firm. Serve mounded on a chop plate and garnish with two hard-cooked eggs. Serves eight.

Though the recipe calls for a whole chicken, this is also a good way to use up leftover chicken. For half this recipe allow at least one cup of chopped chicken.

Chicken and Rice Pilau

1 roasting chicken
1 to 2 teaspoons curry powder
Salt
2 cups uncooked rice
¼ cup butter

Prepare the chicken as for roasting, but without stuffing. Roast, adding a cup of water with which the curry powder has been mixed to the roasting pan and basting frequently to prevent the chicken from becoming dry and to extract the juices. Add more water as needed. At the same time boil the rice in salted water until tender. When the chicken is nicely browned — about half an hour before the chicken is done — turn the rice into the roasting pan and add the butter. Remove the chicken from the pan for a minute, mix the gravy (there should be about two cups), rice and butter and spread the rice smoothly over the bottom of the pan so that a nice crust may form. Replace the chicken and cover the roasting pan.

When the rice has a brown crust on the bottom

dish it up, smothering the chicken in the rice and placing the crust on top. If you have used curry no other seasoning is needed except salt. If, however, you do not care for the curry flavor, or for a variation, season with black pepper and onion to taste, adding the seasonings to the gravy at the beginning of the cooking.

—Mrs. J. R. Sparkman,
Dirleton Plantation, South Carolina

Carolina Pilau

The original recipe reads: "Boil one and a half pounds of bacon; when nearly done add one quart rice; then put in two young fowls and season with salt and pepper."

To serve six we used the following ingredients:

¾ pound bacon
2 cups rice
4 cups water
1 broiler
Salt and pepper

Boiling the bacon gives, of course, a limp product and one rather too greasy for our taste. Instead we cut the bacon in dice and fried it. Then the bacon was removed from the fat, part of the drippings turned off and the rice added and browned slightly. The boiling water was then added, and as soon as the rice was boiling, the chicken, cut as for fricassee, was put in. The water was liberally salted, the pot covered, and the fire lowered so that the rice continued boiling, but not too vigorously. At the end of twenty-five minutes the rice and chicken were both tender and the water had all been absorbed. A seasoning of salt and pepper was added — all pilaus should be highly seasoned — and the bacon again stirred in.

French Pilau I

Charles Cotesworth Pinckney is a great name in American history. One of the name was the president of the Provincial Congress of the American Colonies and another was a general on Washington's staff, and chairman of the committee to frame the American Constitution. It is from this family that we get the first recipe given below for French pilau.

1 3-pound fowl
Salt and pepper
2 cups uncooked rice
¼ cup butter
1 cup blanched almonds
1 cup white raisins
¼ teaspoon curry powder

Have the chicken cut into pieces for serving and boil it gently in water to which salt and pepper have been added. When the chicken is tender, remove it from the broth. There should be about four cups of the chicken stock. To this add the rice, cover it tightly, and let it cook until the rice is tender — about half an hour.

Add the butter to the hot rice and then stir in the other ingredients.

In serving, put the rice first upon the dish and then lay the fowl, which has been kept warm, upon it. This is a delicious dish for Sunday night supper served with Virginia ham, hot biscuits, French peas and coffee, with charlotte russe for dessert.

—*Mrs. Charles Cotesworth Pinckney,*
Runnymede on the Ashley

French Pilau II

Boil a pair of young fowls; when done, take them out and put your rice in the same water, first taking out some liquor. When the rice is done, butter it well, cover the bottom of your dish with half of it, then put the fowls on it and add the remainder of the liquor. Cover the fowls with the other half of the rice, make it smooth and spread over it the yolks of two eggs, well beaten. Bake in a moderate oven.

The proportions in the recipe were rather indefinite but we found that to serve four to six persons the following ingredients were required:

1 small chicken
2 cups rice
1 egg yolk
Salt and pepper
$\frac{1}{3}$ cup butter

Parboil the chicken until tender. Cook the rice until tender in four cups of well-salted chicken broth. When the rice is cooked, add the butter and season to taste with salt and pepper. Place a layer of the rice in the bottom of a well-buttered baking dish and add the pieces of chicken. Cover with the remaining rice, smooth the top and spread with the well-beaten egg yolk. Bake in a moderate oven (350 degrees F.) for about half an hour to brown the top of the dish.

— *Carolina Housewife*

Jambalayah (a Creole Dish)

It would seem at first glance that the cooking of New Orleans and that of Charleston should be very much alike. I am puzzled to know why the two are so different. Both were settled by the French. Both had Negro cooks and both drew from their own neighborhoods shellfish and game. I think the difference may lie in the fact that New Orleans cooking was so heavily influenced by Spain, which left

South Carolina untouched. Occasionally, however, one finds a New Orleans dish that came to South Carolina and was adapted there. The best one of these is Jambalayah.

1 to 1½ cups cold chicken, veal or mutton
1 cup boiled rice
1½ cups stewed tomatoes
1 large onion
1 green pepper
1 large stalk celery
Salt and pepper
Buttered crumbs

Mix the first three ingredients together and let cook for about ten minutes on top of the stove. Then add the onion, green pepper and celery, each vegetable having been chopped. Turn the mixture into a baking dish and cover with buttered crumbs. Bake in a moderately hot oven (375 degrees F.) for one hour. Serve very hot. Serves four and is an excellent way of making a small amount of leftover meat or chicken do double duty.

Red Rice

½ pound bacon
1 small can tomatoes
1 pound rice
Salt and pepper to taste
4 cups chicken broth

Have the bacon sliced and cut in small pieces. Fry it until crisp and remove the bits of bacon. Leave about four tablespoons of the drippings and in this brown the rice, stirring constantly to see that it does not burn. Then add the tomatoes, a teaspoon of salt and the chicken stock. Cover closely and cook for half an hour or until the rice is tender. Add the bacon bits and serve, seasoning to taste with salt and pepper.

— *Sally Washington's Recipe*

Hopping John

South Carolinians, like my husband, who have been away from home a long time, if they feel a culinary homesickness, always long for something called Hopping John, with the accent on the John. This substantial dish is as characteristic of South Carolina as are baked beans of Massachusetts. Indeed, it is a dish which performs the same functions. It is made with what are known in the South as cow peas. It may be impossible to secure these in the North, but black beans might be substituted for the cow peas.

Lettie Gay says of this dish: "We were able to get the cow peas (which look to us far more like beans than peas!) and Hopping John was made. For our tastes the dish seemed a bit flavorless and rather starchy, but seasonings may be added and it should be served accompanied with a green salad."

2 cups cow peas
1 cup uncooked rice
3 cups water in which peas were cooked
3 tablespoons bacon drippings
Salt to taste

Boil the peas until they are tender. Add the rice and bacon drippings and enough of the water in which the peas were boiled to steam the rice (about three cups). Cook over a slow fire for one hour. This serves six.

—*Mrs. T. J. Woodward*

Peas and Rice Pilau
(A Variant of Hopping John)

1 quart cow peas
1½ pounds strip bacon
3 quarts water
Salt
1 quart rice

Boil the peas, bacon and water together, adding salt to taste, until the peas are soft. Then add the boiled or steamed rice (each grain should be separate and dry). Cook the mixture all together for a few minutes and turn onto a large flat dish, putting the bacon on top.

Cheese Toast

8 rounds buttered bread
½ pound American cheese
¼ teaspoon paprika
½ teaspoon Worcestershire sauce

Make a paste of the cheese, which should be fresh, and add the seasonings. Spread the rounds generously with the cheese mixture and set in a hot oven until brown. Serve hot. The cheese toast is especially nice for Sunday night suppers.

— *William's Recipe*

Macaroni Pie

½ pound macaroni
1 tablespoon butter
1 egg, well beaten
1 teaspoon salt
1 teaspoon mustard
1 teaspoon each black and red pepper
2 cups grated cheese
½ cup milk

Boil the macaroni in salted water until tender. Drain; stir in the butter and egg. Mix the mustard with a tablespoon of hot water and add it with the other seasonings. Add the cheese and milk, mix well and turn into a buttered baking dish. Bake in a moderate oven (350 degrees F.)

until the cheese is melted and the dish brown on top, about half an hour.

—*Martha Laurens Patterson*

Eggs Fricassee

The name of Heyward rings down through the history of South Carolina. Thomas Heyward was a signer of the Declaration of Independence. Today its most distinguished member is Du Bose Heyward, author of "Porgy." By a curious coincidence, this recipe is given us by a Heyward whose plantation was burned by the British and who married a Grimball, whose plantation was burned by the Spaniards.

3 hard-cooked eggs
2 tablespoons butter
2 slices toast
1 cup medium white sauce
6 slices bacon or boiled ham
Salt and pepper

Slice the eggs and brown them in the butter. Cook the bacon or use small slices of boiled ham and arrange on the toast. Lay the browned eggs on top of the meat and pour the well-seasoned white sauce over all. This makes an excellent luncheon dish. Serves two.

—*Panchita Heyward Grimball, Wappaoolah Plantation, Cooper River*

Corn Pie

1 cup drained corn
2 egg yolks
2 tablespoons butter
Salt and pepper
1 cup strained tomatoes
1 pound veal

Mix the corn (fresh corn may be used) with the other ingredients except the meat. The veal should be cooked and well seasoned. Put half of the corn mixture into a well-buttered baking dish, add the veal cut in pieces of serving size, and cover with the remainder of the corn and tomatoes. Bake in a moderate oven (350 degrees F.) for about half an hour. This serves four.

Cooked chicken, slices of ham or other meat or shrimp may be substituted for the veal in making this dish.

— *Southern Cook Book*

Okra, Corn and Green Peppers

4 slices salt pork
2 cups sliced okra
3 cups corn
2 sliced green peppers
2 tablespoons flour
$\frac{2}{3}$ cup milk
Salt

Fry until brown the four slices of "white pork." Add the okra, corn and green peppers. Then dredge in the flour and stir until thoroughly mixed. Add the milk and let the mixture come to the boiling point. Season with salt and cook until the peppers are tender. Serve hot.

This may appear as a vegetable, or, served on toast, would make an excellent luncheon dish. Sufficient for eight servings.

—*Mrs. H. A. Woodward,*
Augusta, Georgia

Egg Pie

We are not prepared to say whether this most resembles a custard or a soufflé. Certainly it violates the rules of egg cookery, yet it still remains delicious!

1 tablespoon butter
5 tablespoons flour
1 quart milk, scalded
5 eggs, separated
1 teaspoon salt

Rub the butter and flour together and pour on the scalded milk, taking care that it is perfectly smooth. Beat the egg yolks with the salt and add to the milk and flour batter. Beat well and add the egg whites, beaten stiff. Bake in a hot oven (though this is heresy!) (400 degrees F.) for thirty-five minutes and serve at once, as it will fall if allowed to stand.

This amount will serve eight. Chopped ham added to the recipe is marvelous! Allow about one cup of ham and decrease the salt if necessary.

—*Marie Heyward*

Potage au Macaroni

$\frac{1}{4}$ pound macaroni
3 cups stock or water
3 bouillon cubes (if water is used)
Parmesan cheese

Break the macaroni into short pieces and throw it into the stock or water, to which the bouillon cubes should be added, and boil until the macaroni is tender. The broth should be almost all absorbed. Sprinkle the macaroni with grated Parmesan cheese and serve at once. The macaroni will have a very decided flavor of the meat.

—*Carolina Housewife*

POULTRY AND DRESSINGS

If you say the words " south " and " chicken " to most northeners they think of fried chicken. But in Charleston chicken is cooked in many ways.

In the following recipe for a favorite supper dish can be seen the subtle result of applying French cooking methods to our native dishes. The recipe is one of many supplied by William Deas, Mrs. Rhett's butler.

When we started this book of Charleston cooking we first had a talk with William. A stenographer took down his instructions.

Fried Chicken with Corn Cake

(a Favorite Supper Dish)

Select two young chickens weighing two pounds each; cut in pieces for serving. Squeeze a few drops of lemon over each piece of chicken and season with salt and pepper.

Beat two eggs and add one tablespoon of milk. Dip each piece of chicken in this mixture and then roll in flour. Fry the chicken until tender. It is usually best to brown the chicken first, using plenty of fat in the pan, then cover the pan and let the chicken cook over a slow fire until tender.

Remove the chicken from the pan, add three tablespoons of flour to the fat in the pan and blend in one and one-half cups of milk and season to taste with salt and black pepper. Cut into small pieces the chicken livers and gizzards, which have been cooked separately, and add. Part of the liquor in which they were cooked may also be added to the gravy.

Makes eight corn batter cakes. Place two piles on platter with fried chicken, buttering them while hot. Pour the cream chicken gravy over all and serve. This fried chicken seems to be unusually good, and the corn batter cakes add the perfect touch.

— *William's Recipe*

Roast Chicken

William says: "After your chicken has been cleaned and trussed squeeze over it the juice of one lemon. Lay it in the roaster in about one inch of water, and salt to taste. Lay over the chicken four or five strips of white pork (salt pork is the northern name for this). Cut one small red onion fine and scatter over the chicken. Cover and let steam slowly on top of the stove, basting constantly until done. This will take about two hours. Then put in the oven for a few minutes to brown lightly. A stuffing made of two cups, of parched peanuts gives, ground up, a delicious flavor."

We found that chicken cooked in this way was good as to flavor and very tender. However, there seems no reason why the chicken could not be roasted in the oven, using the onion and lemon juice, but decreasing the amount of water. With a covered roaster there could be less basting and the chicken would taste just the same.

White Fricassee

For a century Charleston has had her own ways of preparing fricasseed chicken. As you can see when you glance over these recipes, they are not for any simple household.

It was either a stroke of genius or an accident which is responsible for the anchovies. The following recipe is taken from *The Carolina Housewife*, published in the fifties, and long out of print. As you can see from these ingredients, it was published in a time of flourishing hospitality.

2 broilers or frying chickens
5 cups water
1 blade mace

¼ teaspoon nutmeg
2 anchovies
1 small onion
1 teaspoon salt
Pepper
½ cup sherry or unsweetened sherry extract
1 cup cream
¼ cup butter
¼ cup flour
1 egg yolk
Juice of 1 lemon

Parboil the chickens, and when they are tender remove them from the broth, skin them and cut them in pieces for serving. Return them to the liquor and add the seasonings, including the wine. Stew gently until very tender. Remove the onion and add the cream, the butter and flour well blended, and when this has come to the boiling point add the beaten egg yolk, but do not let it boil. Add the lemon juice, being very careful not to curdle the mixture.

Rich as this sauce is, it is suggested that mushrooms, a few capers and oysters shredded in a little of their own liquor may be added. Serve garnished with toast points.

This chicken dish has a most unusual flavor, for the anchovies "melt," leaving no visible trace but a most elusive taste.

Chicken à la Tartare

Especially just before and after the Revolutionary War the connection between South Carolina and Paris was surprisingly close. Many Charlestonians knew the famous Mme. de Genlis. Her writings filled some ninety volumes. Though she was the "governor" of the children of Louis Philippe, she was an active revolutionist. And besides that she conducted a house famous for its hospitality and its fine food. She had a busy and vivid life. And to some Charlestonians in Paris she gave a recipe which is used in South Carolina to this day.

The recipe reads: "Singe and draw the chickens; let them swell a little before the fire; cut in half and break the bones slightly; soak them in fresh butter melted, into which put a seasoning of parsley, skelion, mushrooms and the smallest shred of garlic, well chopped together with pepper and salt. Let the chickens steep in the butter for a little while, then grate bread crumb over them and broil over a slow fire. Serve them dry or with a clear gravy."

Since our fire is a gas one our procedure was slightly different from that of Mme. de Genlis. Our ingredients were:

1 broiler
¼ pound butter, melted

4 sprigs parsley
2 scallions or 1 small onion
$\frac{1}{4}$ pound mushrooms
$\frac{1}{4}$ clove garlic
Salt and pepper
Bread crumbs

The broiler, which had been singed, cleaned and split, was put into an aluminum frying pan in which the butter had been melted. The parsley, onion, mushrooms and garlic were chopped and added to the butter with a seasoning of salt and pepper. The frying pan was covered and the broiler was allowed to simmer gently for about fifteen minutes, being turned occasionally, so that it would absorb the flavor of the seasonings. Then it was rolled in grated bread crumbs and broiled until well browned. The chicken meat is delicately flavored with the mushroom-garlic-onion-parsley combination and should tempt the appetite of the most critical. The pre-cooking in the butter sauce also prevents any " underdoneness " of the broiler.

Turkey Hash

One memorable April evening we drove through dark and silent roads into the country near Columbia to a plantation party given by Dr. E. C. Adams. Dr. Adams modestly says that his famous sketches published under the title *Nigger to Nig-*

ger all came to him from his colored man Tad. Tad has so many talents that one does not know which to mention first. He says he is sixty-six, but with his reddish hair, vigorous face and strong, square figure, he appears to be no more than forty-five. He sings; he dances; he has an almost telepathic understanding of the human mind, whether it be that of a white or of a black. And besides all these things he cooks.

There were a dozen Negroes around the place, serving, cooking, singing and dancing, and every few minutes Dr. Adams would shout into the kitchen: "Stop that cooking and come in and sing something!" So the Negroes would shift back and forth, to their own perfect delight, from cooking to dancing, from singing to serving.

I shall never forget the supper served that night, while we wandered from the firelight within to the tree-shadowed lawn without. And of all the incredible dishes served that evening, turkey hash was the most distinguished. It is an insult to South Carolina cooks to think that turkey hash should be made only from leftovers. In the first place, in a large southern house with negro servants, you have no leftovers; and in the second place, to make turkey hash as here given it is vastly worth while to cook a turkey specially for the purpose. As is proper in such dishes, the quantities are not definite in amount. You can vary them according to your own taste.

If there is turkey gravy, use that; but if not, make a sauce of:

- 2 tablespoons butter
- 2 tablespoons flour
- ½ cup cream
- ¾ cup veal stock

Cut the turkey in pieces, not very small, and remove all the skin. Put the turkey into the sauce and add the grated rind of one lemon, white pepper and mace to taste, a tablespoon of mushroom catsup (¼ pound of sautéed mushrooms may be substituted) and let the "hash" simmer for a few minutes. The turkey should be heated through but it must not cook too long or it will be toughened. Oysters added to this make it a practically new dish and also make it go farther.

Pecan Turkey Stuffing

In 1672 a Henry Hughes and some others surrendered land so that the town of Charleston might be built. Perhaps there is some esoteric connection between that and the fact that Mr. Edward Hughes has the most spacious garden and house in the city limits today. Distinguished guests go back to New York and Paris and London boasting to their friends about the pressed turkey and pecan of which they partook in Mr. Hughes' house. For this is more than a mere food; it is a confection. Mr. Hughes allowed us to copy the recipe from his mother's old notebook.

To the recipe was appended a note which read, "The most delicious stuffing that has ever been made. A choice old Charleston recipe." We see no reason to dispute this proclamation. This stuffing is especially good for boned turkey, and is, of course, only for the very greatest of state occasions.

1 turkey liver
12 slices toasted bread
¼ cup butter
3 tablespoons lard
1 teaspoon salt
1 teaspoon black pepper
1 teaspoon celery seed, crushed
1 teaspoon dried Nabob thyme
1 tablespoon parsley, chopped fine
½ nutmeg, grated
6 hard-cooked eggs
¼ teaspoon ground mace
2 cups salted pecans, chopped
1 can mushrooms, chopped fine
½ cup sherry
1 large onion
1 tablespoon lard

Boil the liver the day before the stuffing is made. Roll the toasted bread on a biscuit board, then sift through a colander into a large bowl and add the butter, lard, salt, black pepper, celery seed, thyme, parsley, and grated nutmeg. Pour in a little boiling water and mix thoroughly by hand. Add the whites of the hard-cooked eggs, riced, and the yolks rubbed smooth with the mace. Then add the salted pecans, mushrooms and sherry. Mix together thoroughly.

Put the onion, grated or finely minced, into a frying pan with the lard. When very hot, add the powdered liver and fry until brown. Allow to cool and then mix thoroughly with the other ingredients. Stuff the turkey, having first rubbed it with salt and black pepper both inside and outside.

—*Edward H. Hughes*

Pigeon Pie

4 squabs
Rich pastry
½ cup butter
3 tablespoons flour
1 cup milk
Salt and pepper

Parboil the squabs until they are tender. Cut them in half and fry them until they are brown. Line a deep casserole with rich pastry and place the fried squabs in it. To the stock in which the squabs were cooked (there should be about three cups) add the butter and flour, blended together, and the milk. Season to taste with salt and pepper and pour over the squabs.

Two-inch squares of pastry may be added to the pie for dumplings. Cover with a top crust of pastry and bake in a hot oven (400 degrees F.) for forty-five minutes. This makes eight servings.

Mulacolong

The marching rhythm of this name is entrancing. Its origin is as mysterious as the flavor of the dish itself.

A bird which has reached the age politely spoken of as "uncertain" may serve as the *pièce de résistance* of any dinner and reflect glory on the hostess if it is prepared in this manner. Young chickens may also be cooked in the same way by using somewhat less veal stock and reducing the time of cooking.

1 fowl
1 large onion, chopped
3 pints veal stock
1 tablespoon lemon juice
1 teaspoon turmeric
Salt and pepper

Cut the fowl in pieces and fry it until it is well browned. Then add the chopped onion to the fat and allow this to brown also. Add the veal stock, which should be very strong, and the turmeric mixed with the lemon juice. Season with salt and pepper and cook until the chicken is tender. The stock should cook down so that it forms a rich gravy which should be served over the chicken.

— *Carolina Housewife*

Pressed Chicken

1 3-pound chicken
1 cup chopped celery
5 hard-cooked eggs
$\frac{1}{4}$ teaspoon mustard
Salt and red pepper
1 tablespoon gelatin
2 tablespoons cold water

Boil the chicken gently until the meat easily falls from the bones. Chop the chicken meat fine and add the chopped celery and the hard-cooked eggs, diced. Mix all together, adding the seasonings to taste.

Soak the gelatin in the cold water and dissolve it in the liquor (there should be two cups) in which the chicken was cooked. Let the broth cool and add the chicken mixture. Turn into a mold and set upon ice or in the refrigerator to become firm.

Cut into slices and serve on lettuce leaves, with or without mayonnaise.

Celery seed may be used in place of celery, but we found that the crispness of the vegetable was preferable.

— *Jane Montgomery*

Batter for Chickens

This recipe, contributed by Mary Leize Simons from the old notebook of Miss Elizabeth Harleston, proved to be most delicious, though at first glance it was not very enlightening. It reads: "One pint of milk, one pint of flour, two eggs, a little salt; beat up very light — Yeast Powder."

After experimenting with this batter for deep-fat frying we found that the following amounts would make enough batter to cover a medium-sized chicken.

- 1½ cups flour
- 1 tablespoon baking powder
- ½ teaspoon salt
- 1 egg, well beaten
- ½ cup milk

Mix and sift the dry ingredients. Mix the egg and milk together and combine with the first mixture. Dip each piece of chicken in the batter and fry in deep fat until brown. The chicken must, of course, be cooked until tender before dipping in the batter, since the short time of frying would not cook the chicken.

—*Mary Leize Simons*

STUFFINGS

POULTRY dressings in South Carolina are of great variety. Cornbread and pecan are the most delicious, but peanuts are most commonly used. In parts of the state these are called " goobers," and most farmers grow a patch of them. One of the best-known street criers of Charleston used to be the " peanut man." Essie Woodward Messervey writes us that for a generation this familiar figure walked the streets near the sea wall, selling his bags of peanuts. Every child knew him. Mrs. Messervey says that the " peanut man " made up his own songs. One of these was:

I'm so glad, I'm so glad,
Old ship o' Zion is passin' by.
Want de time to come
An' I hope I shall be dere,
To see de little niggers
Pourin' 'lasses on his hair.

I'm so glad, I'm so glad,
An' I hope de time will come

An' I hope I shall de dere,
To see de ole ship o' Zion
Takin' de little chillun home.

When he saw her write down the words of this song the "peanut man" asked her:

"Is yo' going to make a story 'bout me, in a book?"

She told him that she would make a story about him, but could not promise that it would ever be a book.

"Missus, I knows a good tale 'bout two slavery niggers. Want to hear dat too?"

And then he told this story:

"'Fore de war dere was two white men dat wuz always tryin' to out-do each other. Dey bof had a man-servant dat dey bragged on all de time. One nigger was named Sambo and de odder Rastus. Rastus' master wouldn' allow dat Sambo was de best servant; he said dat Rastus could tell him anyt'ing he wanted to know. Well Sambo's boss wanted to try dis out and see if Rastus could do it. So he make Sambo go in de woods and cotch a coon fo' him, den he puts de coon in a box and take him over to Rastus' master an' bets him a thousan' dollars dat Rastus can't tell what am in dat box. Rastus' boss calls him an' says, 'Rastus, I has bet dis man a thousan' dollars dat you can tell him what am in dat box. Now tell him, Rastus.'

"Rastus he stan' dere and t'ink and t'ink but he ain't know what am in dat box. Finally he got to say somethin' so he make up he mind to tell de trut' and he say, 'Massah, yo's cotch de ole coon at last.' And fore he could say he ain't know what am in de box, Sambo's boss t'row de money down an' say, 'How de debbil did yo' know dare was a coon in dat box?'"

Charming as the "peanut man" was, Mrs. Rhett suggests that in every one of the recipes the flavor of pecans will be found better than that of peanuts. South Carolina and Georgia are the land of the large soft-shelled pecan, and they are freely and most successfully used in delicate cooking.

Lettie Gay says that the walnut, so common that it isn't fully appreciated and little used except in Waldorf salad, has a more telling flavor in cookery than any other nut. Although its flavor is, fortunately, not as pervasive as that of the peanut, it retains its crisp nut-like quality even after cooking.

Aiken County Corn Bread Dressing

Dramatic contrast separates the upper part of South Carolina from the marshes around Charleston. Aiken County, now the resort of northerners rich enough to own stables of horses, is a land of hills and tall ship-mast pines. This recipe, calling for white corn meal, a characteristic ingredient of southern cookery, came from Aiken County.

2 cups white corn meal
1 cup flour
2 cups milk
2 tablespoons shortening
2 tablespoons baking powder
1 teaspoon salt
1 onion
2 eggs
Pepper to taste

Make a batter of the cornmeal, flour, salt, baking powder, shortening (the oil from the baking fowl is generally used) and milk. Bake in a hot oven (400 degrees F.) until done, about half an hour. Then crumble the bread, add one medium-sized onion, chopped fine, pepper and a little more salt. Break in the two eggs and wet with the juice from the baking chicken or turkey. The liver chopped fine and added to the dressing improves it, as does the addition of a hard-cooked egg.

After mixing thoroughly, put the mixture on one side of the baking dish and roast with the fowl until brown. When basting the fowl, baste the dressing also to keep it moist and to improve the flavor. This amount will serve twelve persons.

—*Mrs. Cornelius Youmans Reamer,*
Columbia, South Carolina

Oyster Stuffing

1 pint of oysters
4 cups bread crumbs
½ teaspoon salt
¼ teaspoon celery salt
¼ teaspoon paprika

Mix all the ingredients together and stuff the fowl. Roast in the usual manner.

—*Emma Salley, "Pirate House"*

Chicken Dressing

Mix two cups of white corn meal with one teaspoon of salt and water sufficient to make a stiff dough. Bake in a hot griddle as for hoe cake.

Using this corn bread make a dressing using the the following proportions:

3 cups corn bread
3 cups cold crumbled biscuits or toast
1 medium-sized onion, chopped very fine

3 tablespoons butter, melted
Pepper
2 eggs
Chicken stock

Mix the ingredients together, adding enough chicken stock to moisten. Half this amount will be sufficient to stuff a roasting chicken.

—*Mrs. I. E. Salley*

Veal and Chestnut Stuffing

William's recipe, as originally given, reads:

"Cook 1½ pounds veal. Put through meat grinder with

1 pound mushrooms
1 pound chestnuts
1 large onion

"Add ½ cup butter and 2 cups corn bread. Season with black pepper and salt, and stuff turkey, roast chicken, hens, or any kind of poultry."

There is really nothing we need to add except that we found than an even one-half cup of butter, melted, did not furnish quite enough liquid to moisten this amount of dressing. We added a little veal stock to make it of the desired consistency.

The flavor is excellent and the dressing has the crumbly texture which seems characteristic of southern stuffings. This amount will stuff a large-sized turkey. Half of the recipe provided sufficient stuffing to fill a six-pound chicken, with an extra dish of dressing besides.

— *William's Recipe*

Sally Washington's Chicken Dressing

My own cook, Washington, using the usual ingredients for chicken dressing, achieved such a marvelous result that we took our notebook and pencil to her and got her exact measurements. Unlike most Negro cooks, she was able to give us these.

3 cups broken toasted stale bread
1 small onion, chopped
4 tablespoons butter
Milk or water
¼ teaspoon black pepper
½ teaspoon thyme
Salt to taste

Toast about three and one-half rather thick slices of stale bread and break into small pieces. Dampen with milk or water so that the bread crumbs are soft but not mushy. Melt two tablespoons of butter in a frying pan and mix with the bread. Season with the pepper, thyme and salt. Melt the remaining butter and fry the onions in it until they are brown. Then add the bread and let it brown, stirring frequently.

This amount will stuff one five-pound chicken. Sautéing the dressing gives it an unusual flavor which is well worth the extra effort in preparation.

Peanut Dressing

2 cups shelled peanuts
1½ cups toasted bread crumbs
2 tablespoons melted butter
1 egg yolk
Broth from fowl

The peanuts should be crisply parched, which means that usually they will need to be put into the oven and crisped somewhat before using. Grind the peanuts and add the bread crumbs, melted butter and egg yolk. The original recipe calls for no liquid, but we found it necessary to moisten the dressing somewhat with broth obtained by cooking the neck and giblets of the fowl. We also seasoned the dressing with salt and pepper.

If the chicken is very fat leave out the butter, as there is plenty of fat in the peanuts. This dressing is a favorite in Charleston for chicken and turkey. For turkey double the recipe.

Corn Bread Stuffing

Break up enough corn bread to make four cups and add one chopped onion and one cup of celery and season with salt and pepper. Beat five eggs slightly and stir into the corn bread mixture. Mix thoroughly and stuff the chicken. Make a roll of the leftover stuffing and place in the roasting pan with the chicken. Baste this stuffing each time the chicken is basted.

This stuffing, thoroughly cooked with the gravy outside the chicken, is considered by many the best part of the dish. This stuffing may also be used for turkey.

— *William's Recipe*

MEATS

Patience Pennington

To those who have read that glowing book, *The Woman Rice Planter*, it will be a special delight to get recipes from the kitchen of its author. Patience Pennington died on her plantation, Chicora Wood, in 1921. Before her marriage she was an Alston, and the history of that family is surrounded by glamour. Theodosia, the beautiful, brilliant daughter of Aaron Burr, and probably the only person whom he ever loved, was the wife of Governor Joseph Alston of South Carolina. Rumor says she set out from her plantation near Chicora Wood on her last dreadful journey, when she set sail from Charleston to visit her father in New York. Neither she nor the ship was ever heard of again. It is thought that she was captured by pirates, but it is hoped that the ship sank in a storm.

We owe the four following rare recipes to Mrs. Charles Albert Hill, who inherited them from her sister, Patience Pennington.

Stewed Oxtail

This makes a very delicious main course for a cold day. By increasing the amount of stock or water, the recipe might serve as the basis of an oxtail soup, always a favorite with the men of the family.

3 oxtails
Flour
3 cups soup stock
½ teaspoon black pepper
½ teaspoon Cayenne pepper
10 whole allspice
Bunch of savory herbs
½ teaspoon Worcestershire sauce

Have the oxtails cut in pieces of serving size. Roll the pieces in flour and put into a saucepan with a tightly fitting cover. Add the soup stock (water and bouillon cubes may be substituted) and seasonings, except the Worcestershire sauce. For the herbs we used a bunch of soup greens consisting of celery, parsley, a leek and a carrot. Stew slowly for two and a half to three hours. Add the Worcestershire sauce and serve very hot. This recipe serves six.

—*Mrs. Charles Albert Hill*
(*from Patience Pennington*)

Beef Olives

Round steak prepared in this manner becomes very appetizing. The "olives" are kin to "veal birds" but the meat in this case is stuffed only with bacon and seasonings.

1 pound round steak
1 medium-sized onion
1 tablespoon chopped parsley
¼ teaspoon allspice
1 teaspoon salt
¼ teaspoon pepper
Flour
Bacon
⅔ cup stock or water
1 teaspoon vinegar
1 teaspoon catsup

Have the round steak sliced very thin. Pound it with a rolling pin and dust with flour. Mix the seasonings well together, having the onion chopped fine. Cut the meat in strips which will accommodate about half a slice of bacon, and place a piece of bacon and some of the seasonings on each piece of meat. Roll each piece up and tie it with thin cord or coarse thread. Place in a roasting pan, close together, and pour over the "olives" the water or stock seasoned with the vinegar and catsup. Bake in a slow oven (300 degrees F.) in a covered pan for about two hours. Then remove the cords and serve with a gravy made from the liquid in the pan. Serves four.

—*Mrs. Charles Albert Hill*
(from Patience Pennington)

Galantine of Chicken

Dissolve 1 ounce of gelatin in ¼ pint of cold water. Let stand for half an hour, then add 1 pint of boiling water (or stock), ¾ teaspoon of vinegar, salt and ¼ teaspoon of Cayenne. Cut veal, or chicken, into small pieces, enough to make one cup. Put meat into small molds if for salad or large molds if for serving whole, add a few capers in each mold and pour the gelatin over. Set on ice to harden and turn out on lettuce leaves and minced celery.

—*Mrs. Charles Albert Hill*
(from Patience Pennington)

Beef à la Mode

6 pounds round of beef
3 large onions, minced
1 teaspoon whole black pepper
1 teaspoon whole allspice
1 teaspoon salt
¾ pound bacon
½ cup vinegar

Pound the pepper and allspice in a mortar or grind in a pepper grinder. If this is not possible, use two teaspoons of the ground seasonings in place of the one teaspoon each of whole spice. With a sharp knife cut gashes in the beef about two inches apart and fill with the seasoning of pepper, allspice, salt and minced onion, all well mixed together, and the bacon cut in strips an inch square on the end and as long as the beef. Bind the meat tightly with tape to keep the seasonings in, put in a roasting pan, pour over it the vinegar mixed with two cups of water, cover and roast for three hours or until the meat is tender. The oven should be slow (300 degrees F.).

—*Mrs. Charles Albert Hill*
(*from Patience Pennington*)

Barbecued Ham

6 slices boiled ham
2 tablespoons butter
1 tablespoon vinegar
$\frac{1}{4}$ teaspoon dry mustard
Pepper and salt to taste

Brown the ham slightly in the butter. Mix the mustard, salt, pepper and vinegar together; pour over the ham and butter and cook for a minute or two. Serve very hot.

This is an easy way of preparing ham so that

it will seem different and appetizing even when ham must be featured on the bill of fare several times in rather close succession.

—Mrs. Cornelius Youmans Reamer

Smothered Veal

One-dish meals are by no means a modern invention. This recipe, handed down by an early Charlestonian who received it from Madame de Genlis, contains meat, potatoes, and vegetables, and they are all cooked in the same dish.

3 pounds veal
3 slices bacon
Roasted chestnuts
Potatoes
Carrots
Turnips
Onions
Celery root
1 sprig thyme
1 sprig parsley
3 cups stock

Place the veal in a Dutch oven or waterless cooker and put the strips of bacon over it. Cover the bacon with the chestnuts and vegetables. The amounts used depend entirely upon personal taste. The veal must be covered entirely—that is the only rule. Moisten with the stock, cover and cook over a slow fire until the meat is tender — about two hours.

A knuckle of veal is the piece usually purchased for this dish. This will serve eight if there is a plentiful supply of vegetables.

Scrapple

Lettie Gay says after testing this recipe:

" When we first looked at the scrapple after it had been allowed to cool, we were most unfavorably impressed. It had a greyish look and seemed most uninviting. One taste changed our feeling toward it entirely! This is a most delicious dish, one which might well compete with pâté de fois gras as a canapé spread. The flavor is delicate and quite delightful. Although we did not try sealing the scrapple in half-pint jars, there seems no reason why this could not be done successfully, making a product which would keep for several weeks at least."

To make the scrapple, take the head, liver, and feet of a hog and boil them until the flesh drops from the bones — about two and a half hours. Grind the meat and season with red and black pepper, adding salt to taste.

Make a cornmeal mush of one cup of cornmeal and three cups of the stock. Add the meat and mix well. Cook in the top of a double boiler or in a pan set in another pan of water for about half an hour. If the scrapple seems too stiff, a little more of the liquor may be added. It should be stiff enough to cut when cold. Mold in oblong pans. This may be cut in slices, rolled in flour, and sautéed before serving.

— *Marie H. Heyward, Wappaoolah Plantation, Cooper River*

Larded Liver

2 pounds calf's liver, left whole
½ pound fat salt pork
1 cup mustard sauce
2 cups water
1 tablespoon salt
½ teaspoon black pepper
1 onion, chopped fine

Wipe the liver well with a damp cloth. Cut several incisions through the thickness of the liver and insert in them narrow strips of the pork and bits of chopped onion. Place in a heavy saucepan or Dutch oven, add the water and seasonings and bring to the boiling point. Baste with mustard sauce taken from a bottle of mustard pickle or chow chow. Let simmer until the meat is tender — about an hour and a half. Brown the outside of the liver in a little fat and serve with a gravy made of the liquor in the pan. This may also be served cold. Two pounds of liver will serve eight generously. Slice before serving.

— *William's Recipe*

Virginia Ham

This recipe was in household use by Mrs. Henry Newman, mother of the famous writer, Frances Newman, author of *The Hard-Boiled Virgin.*

After scrubbing the ham thoroughly, put it to soak in tepid water overnight. Cover with cold water in the morning and bring it to the boiling point. When the water begins to boil, lower the flame, or, if cooked over a coal fire, push the kettle to the back of the stove and let it continue to simmer until well done. For a fourteen-pound ham, allow six and one-half hours for cooking. Let the ham remain in the water in which it has boiled until it is quite cold. Then skin the ham and cover with cracker crumbs and brown sugar mixed in equal parts and seasoned with black pepper. Stick the ham with cloves and bake in a moderately hot oven (375 degrees F.) until the crust is brown, from one-half to three-quarters of an hour.

— *Mrs. Henry Newman*

Mutton Hash

The original recipe reads: "Take a leg of mutton half-roasted, cut it in thin slices and put it into a stew pan with a ladle full of strong broth, half a pint of claret, a bunch of sweet herbs, three anchovies, an onion, spice and salt. Set it on the fire and let it stew two hours. Put in half a pint of oyster liquor a little before it is served up, and garnish with sausages and sliced lemon."

While this is a bit too complicated and expensive to attempt, it is possible to make a "hash" of leftover lamb or mutton which will not compare unfavorably with it. Make a sauce, using either gravy or bouillon cubes and adding one-fourth cup sherry flavoring, three anchovies, a little thyme and marjoram, a finely minced onion, nutmeg and mace and salt to taste. Let this simmer until well blended — about fifteen minutes — and add sliced cold meat. Heat the meat through and serve at once garnished with slices of lemon and toast points. The oyster liquor may be added if on hand, but the flavor that it gives is so delicate that it is hardly recognizable.

Veal or Venison Paté

2 pounds lean veal or venison
1 pound fat salt pork
1 egg
1 cup bread crumbs
1 large can mushrooms
Salt, pepper and nutmeg to taste

Chop the meat fine (it is better to have the butcher chop the meat at the shop) and see that it is free from strings. Put the mushrooms through the meat grinder or chop them fine. Mix all the ingredients together well and mold in loaf form. Roll in additional bread crumbs, put into a well-greased baking dish and bake in a moderately hot oven (375 degrees F.) until thoroughly done, about an hour and a quarter. A little water should be put in the baking dish with the meat and the loaf should be basted from time to time during cooking.

For the jelly to be poured over the cold patty use:

1½ tablespoons gelatin
½ cup cold water
3 bouillon cubes
1½ cups boiling water

Soak the gelatin in the cold water for five minutes. Dissolve the bouillon cubes and soaked gelatin in the boiling water and add additional seasoning if necessary. Let it cool until it begins to thicken. When the patty is cold, pour the jelly into a mold and reverse the patty in it, that is, place the top of the patty in the bottom of the mold so that it will be right side up when turned out. Allow the gelatin mixture to stand in the refrigerator until firm, and turn out. Serve in slices.

—Mrs. E. H. Sparkman
(from Mr. George F. Babbage)

Rice Pie

3 cups boiled rice
2 tablespoons butter
Leftover beef stew or
cold meat with gravy
2 hard-cooked eggs

Have the rice boiled in salted water until soft, and while still warm mix the butter with it. Another tablespoon or two of butter may be added to make it a bit richer, if desired. Line a casserole with the buttered rice, turn in the leftover stew or cold meat with gravy, having the meat well seasoned, and cover with rice. The hard-cooked eggs may be added to the meat part of the dish cut either in slices or diced.

Bake in a moderately hot oven (375 degrees F.) until the rice is browned on top — about twenty-five minutes. A raw egg may be added to the rice and butter for a variation. This is an excellent way of serving second-day stew, which has always been a problem.

—*Carolina Housewife*

SWEET POTATOES, RICE AND GREEN VEGETABLES

If you ask for potatoes in the South you get sweet potatoes. When you want the white tuber of the North you must ask for Irish potatoes. But once you have tasted some of Charleston's sweet potato dishes you will never again even think of white potatoes.

Southern cooks also make a distinction between yams and sweet potatoes. Charleston housewives specify the yam whenever they can get it — a moist, luscious, orange-colored tuber, much more exotic looking than the light-yellow sweet potato usual in New York, with its dry, mealy texture. All of these recipes are applicable to either type of potato, but more liquid is usually required in cooking the dry yellow kind. The light-colored sweet potato was used in standardizing all of the recipes given below, the richer yams being inaccessible in most northern markets.

If you boil a sweet potato in its skin, or "candy" it, it is good, but is not distinguished. But if you follow a Charleston recipe the result is likely to have the complicated simplicity that distinguishes a masterpiece. Nor is the dish necessarily a difficult one to prepare.

There is, for instance, that supremely good sweet-potato dish which was donated to this collection of Charleston recipes by Miss Leize Dawson, the fragile owner of the Villa Margherita. The Villa deserves to have an entire book written about its cookery, which has won for it an international reputation. It is, for some strange reason, better known in Europe than it is in this country. It is a quiet, restricted little hotel looking out over a park of live oaks and palmettos which curves along the edge of a blue bay. An occasional white-winged ship comes down this quiet bay, an occasional steamer crosses at a distance. But wild birds, ducks and gulls and little sandpipers, are busy over it all day long.

A good cook can usually guess at the main constituents of a given dish, but the one given below has a subtle something in its seasoning which defies recognition until you are told the recipe. And then you will be astonished, as we all were, at its simplicity.

Sweet Potatoes Margherita

Slice five boiled sweet potatoes and arrange in layers in a buttered baking dish, alternating with brown sugar, dots of butter and slices of orange with the peel left on. Add enough water to make a thick syrup. Be careful not to add too much water, for the syrup should be quite rich. Bake in a moderate oven (350 degrees F.) for one hour, basting occasionally with the syrup in the dish.

This is especially nice to serve with duck or game. Slices of lemon may be mixed with the orange, or lemon only may be used if preferred.

—*Leize Dawson, Villa Margherita*

Sweet Potato Croquettes

2 cups mashed sweet potatoes
2 tablespoons butter
1 tablespoon salt
2 tablespoons brown sugar
¼ teaspoon white pepper
Egg
Crumbs

Bake sweet potatoes until they are tender; then scoop out the centers and put them through a potato ricer. (Boiled sweet potatoes, mashed, may be used, although the flavor is not so delicate as with the baked ones.) Add the butter, salt, sugar and pepper to the mashed sweet potatoes and beat them in well. Form the potatoes into small cylinders, dip in egg and then in crumbs and fry in deep fat until golden brown.

This amount will make twelve cylinders. This is supposed to be six servings, but we predict that most people will claim more than one serving.

—*William's Recipe*

Sweet Potato Pone I

For the main course:

3 large raw sweet potatoes
1 pint boiling water
1 teaspoon salt
1 teaspoon black pepper
1 tablespoon allspice
$\frac{1}{4}$ cup butter
Sugar to taste

Pare and grate the raw sweet potatoes. Add the boiling water and mix well. Add the rest of the ingredients (we found one-fourth cup of brown sugar about the right amount for our taste) and stir until thoroughly mixed. Then turn into a buttered shallow pan and bake in a moderate oven (350 degrees F.) until brown, about an hour.

The allspice goes excellently with the sweet potato, but if you are not fond of this spice we recommend decreasing the amount suggested to two teaspoons. Serves eight.

Sweet Potato Pone II

For the main course:

2 medium-sized sweet potatoes
1 pint cold water
4 tablespoons brown sugar
3 tablespoons butter
½ teaspoon ginger
¼ teaspoon salt

Peel and grate the raw sweet potatoes. Add the other ingredients and mix thoroughly. Turn into a buttered baking dish and bake in a moderate oven (350 degrees F.) for about three hours. Serves four.

— *Miss Ethel Norvell*

Sweet Potato Pone III

Either dessert or main dish:

1 pint grated raw sweet potato
1 cup sugar
½ cup milk
½ cup butter
1 teaspoon ginger
1 tablespoon molasses (optional)
⅛ teaspoon cinnamon
⅛ teaspoon nutmeg
Juice of ½ lemon
Grated rind of 1 lemon

Mix the ingredients well together and turn into a shallow baking pan which has been well buttered. Bake in a moderate oven (350 degrees F.) for one hour. Serves eight.

— *Mrs. Pinckney*

Sweet Potato Pone IV

The original recipe serves sixteen, so we used one-fourth of the amounts called for. The revised recipe requires:

½ pound sweet potatoes, grated
5 tablespoons butter
½ cup brown sugar
½ teaspoon salt
Ginger to taste
½ cup water

Cream the butter and sugar, add the salt and ginger and stir in the sweet potatoes and water. Bake in a moderate oven (325 degrees F.) in a buttered baking dish for about forty-five minutes.

— *Mary Leize Simons (from old kitchen notebook of Bossis Plantation)*

Sweet Potato Pone (a Dessert) I

2 cups grated raw sweet potato
½ cup maple syrup
2½ teaspoons powdered ginger

½ cup sugar
1 teaspoon grated orange rind
½ cup butter, melted

Mix the ingredients thoroughly together and turn into a buttered baking dish. Bake in a moderate oven (325 degrees F.) for about one and a half hours. This sometimes takes longer, due to the difference in the potatoes. Serve with hard sauce, preferably one flavored with wine, and sprinkled with grated nutmeg after piling on the serving plate. Recipe serves six.

—*Mrs. P. C. Kirk, Loch Dhu Plantation*

Sweet Potato Pone (a Ginger Dessert) II

1 cup grated raw sweet potato
2 eggs
½ cup sugar
¼ cup molasses
½ cup milk
½ tablespoon ginger

Add the eggs to the sweet potato and beat well; add the remaining ingredients and beat until thoroughly mixed. Turn the mixture into a buttered baking dish and bake in a moderate oven (350 degrees F.) for about an hour.

The eggs and lack of butter give this pudding a firmer and less buttery rich texture. This should be an especially popular pudding with ginger devotees. Six servings.

— *William's Recipe*

Sweet Potato Pone (a Dessert) III

This recipe for a spicy dessert, used for generations on the Bluff Plantation, Cooper River, calls for " one wine glass of orange or rose brandy," but since our supply shelf did not yield either of these ingredients we substituted sherry flavoring and rosewater with good results. The recipe, as given below, is one-fourth of the original quantities.

¼ cup brown sugar
¼ cup butter
1 cup raw grated sweet potato
1½ tablespoons sherry flavoring
½ tablespoon rosewater
⅛ teaspoon each of mace, nutmeg and cinnamon
1 tablespoon ginger
½ cup molasses
¼ cup milk
1 ounce citron or orange preserves

Cream the butter and sugar together, add the grated sweet potato, flavorings, molasses and milk. Beat well and stir in the preserves. Turn into a buttered pudding dish and bake in a moderate oven (350 degrees F.) for about an hour and a quarter. Six servings.

This is a rich pudding with a pronounced ginger flavor. We found that one teaspoon of ginger instead of the tablespoon called for gave a pudding of much more delicate flavor in which the rosewater blended subtly.

—*Miss Charlotte Ball*

Sweet Potato Pudding I
(Variation of Sweet Potato Pone)

⅔ cup grated raw sweet potato
1 tablespoon syrup
⅓ cup brown sugar
1 egg, separated
1 tablespoon butter, melted
⅔ cup milk
⅓ cup water
3 tablespoons each citron, raisins and currants
2 tablespoons flour
⅛ teaspoon each cinnamon, cloves and nutmeg

Rub the syrup and sugar into the grated potato, add the beaten egg yolk, the melted butter, milk and water. Dredge the fruit with the flour and mix in the spices. Add to the first mixture, stirring well. Last of all fold in the stiffly beaten egg white and turn into a well-buttered baking dish. Bake in a moderate oven (350 degrees F.)

for about an hour and a half, and serve hot with hard sauce.

The citron may be omitted and one-fourth cup each of raisins and currants substituted, if preferred.

—*Mrs. E. H. Sparkman*

Sweet Potato Pudding II

Unlike most of the sweet potato puddings, in this recipe from the Harleston family notebook, Bossis Plantation, the potatoes are cooked before being combined with the other ingredients.

- ½ pound sweet potatoes
- ½ pound brown sugar
- ¼ pound butter
- 4 egg yolks
- 2 egg whites
- 1 teaspoon grated nutmeg
- ½ cup sherry

Boil the sweet potatoes and mash while they are hot. Allow them to cool. Cream the butter and sugar together. Add the well-beaten egg yolks, the nutmeg, mashed potatoes and the sherry. Fold in the egg whites and turn into a buttered baking dish. Bake in a moderate oven (350 degrees F.) for about thirty-five minutes. Serve with hard sauce. This will serve six generously.

—*Mary Leize Simons*

Pear Sweet Potatoes

Select small sweet potatoes and boil them until tender, but by no means mushy. Pare and shape each one as much like a pear as possible. Make a syrup of:

1 cup brown sugar
$\frac{1}{3}$ cup water

Boil the sugar and water for a minute or two and then pour it over the pear-shaped potatoes, which have been arranged in a buttered baking pan. Set in a moderately hot oven (375 degrees F.) for about fifteen minutes, basting at least twice. Just before serving stick a bay leaf in the top of each "pear."

—*Leize Dawson, Villa Margherita*

Lemon Sweet Potato Pudding

This sweet potato pudding, unlike others of the same name, is really a dish to accompany meat instead of being a dessert. The flavor of lemon and orange is delicious with the sweet potatoes and is so simple to prepare that it should prove a real favorite. Another point in its favor is that it can be prepared for the oven in the morning and merely reheated for the dinner just before serving time.

6 medium-sized sweet potatoes
6 tablespoons butter
6 tablespoons brown sugar
2 teaspoons grated lemon rind
1 cup orange juice

Boil, peel and mash the sweet potatoes. Add the butter and sugar and stir in well. Then add the lemon rind and orange juice and beat until fluffy. Turn into a well-buttered baking dish and put in a moderate oven (350 degrees F.) for half an hour. The potatoes should be in peaks on top so that they will brown. Serves eight.

—*Leize Dawson, Villa Margherita*

Sweet Potato Pie

This sweet potato pie is a mouth-watering affair in a big, round dish oozing with brown richness.

3 large sweet potatoes
2 eggs, separated
½ teaspoon vanilla
¼ teaspoon ground spice
½ teaspoon salt
4 tablespoons sugar
Pastry

Boil sweet potatoes until tender, then peel and mash them until soft and creamy. Add the yolks of the eggs, the vanilla and spice (we chose cinnamon) and the salt and sugar. Mix well and spread about an inch deep on top of pastry which has been used to line a pie tin. Bake in a quick oven (425 degrees F.) until the crust is brown, about twenty-five minutes.

Make a meringue of the egg whites and remaining sugar and spread over the top of the pie and return to the oven, which should be slow (300 degrees F.) until the meringue is brown. This should be served hot.

This may also be baked in a pudding dish without the pastry.

—*Sally Washington's Recipe*

Sweet Potato Marshmallow Pudding

3 large sweet potatoes
1 egg
2 tablespoons butter
1 cup milk
½ cup seeded raisins
4 tablespoons sugar
12 marshmallows

Boil sweet potatoes until done. Peel and mash until creamy. Add the beaten egg, butter, milk, raisins and sugar. Put into a buttered baking dish and top with the marshmallows. Bake for about ten minutes in a moderate oven (350 degrees F.) or until the marshmallows brown.

Serve at once. This makes from six to eight servings.

—*Leize Dawson, Villa Margherita*

Sweet Potatoes with Apple

6 large apples (tart apples are best)
5 medium-sized sweet potatoes
½ cup butter
1 cup sugar
1 cup hot water

Boil the potatoes until tender, peel and slice in thick pieces. Peel and core the apples and slice like the potatoes. Place a layer of potatoes in the bottom of a baking dish, dot with butter and sprinkle with sugar, then add a layer of apples. Continue alternating potatoes and apples and butter and sugar until all the ingredients are used up. Then pour over all the cup of hot water. Bake in a moderately hot oven (375 degrees F.) about half an hour or until the apples are done.

This dish may be varied by adding cinnamon or by using brown sugar.

—*Mrs. Cornelius Youmans Reamer*

Boiled Rice I

To one pint of rice allow one gallon of cold water. Put in an iron pot and let come to a boil slowly and continue to boil slowly until grains are swollen and soft.

Set back on stove, covered, and let it dry.

One hour is about the time required for this.

— *Essie Woodward Messervy*

Boiled Rice II

Wash one cup of rice in several waters. Have two quarts of water salted and boiling hot. Sift the rice in and boil for thirty minutes. Put it into a strainer, rinse in hot water, and set over a kettle to dry. Serve very hot.

— *William's Recipe*

Rice Croquettes I

2 cups boiled rice
½ cup thick white sauce
1 egg, separated
1 teaspoon salt
3 tablespoons grated American cheese
⅛ teaspoon Cayenne
Bread crumbs

Add to the rice, while hot, the white sauce, well-beaten egg yolk, salt, cheese and Cayenne. Set aside to cool, then mold into balls or cylinders. Dip in the well-beaten white of the egg and roll in bread crumbs. Fry in deep fat and serve while hot. This makes twelve small croquettes.

Rice Croquettes II

Although these are to be served with wild duck according to the recipe, we found them excellent with tame duck as well.

2 cups boiled rice
4 egg yolks
Egg and crumbs
Currant jelly

Have the rice boiled until it is quite soft. Beat the egg yolks into it and cook in the upper part of a double boiler for eight minutes. Turn out on a platter and allow the mixture to cool. Then roll into cylinders and dip these in beaten egg and then in crumbs and fry in deep fat. Drain on brown paper, make a dent in the top of each and fill with currant jelly.

—*Mrs. L. D. Simonds*

Scalloped Cauliflower

1 head cauliflower
1 cup bread crumbs
2 tablespoons melted butter
1 cup milk (about)
1 egg
Salt and pepper to taste

Boil the cauliflower in salted water until tender. Break into flowerets and place them, stems downward, in a buttered baking dish. Beat the bread crumbs to a soft paste with the melted butter and milk. The amount of milk required will depend upon the dryness of the crumbs. Season to taste and whip in the egg. Season the cauliflower with salt and pepper and a little butter if desired and pour the mixture over it. Bake for ten minutes covered in a quick oven (425 degrees F.) and then uncover and bake until brown.

—*Southern Cook Book*

Stewed Cucumbers

It is very seldom that one thinks of serving cucumbers any way except sliced raw. They seem almost like another vegetable stewed, and a very good one, too.

2 large cucumbers
1 medium-sized onion
½ cup vinegar
Salt and pepper to taste
2 tablespoons butter

Cut the peeled cucumbers in one-fourth inch slices, chop the onion, add a little salt and simmer them for twenty minutes, or until very tender. Drain, add the vinegar, salt and pepper to taste, and the butter. Cook for three minutes longer and serve with the sauce.

The sauce may be thickened by adding a little flour; but while this was good, we felt that it was better without the flour.

Broccoli

When, a few years ago, eager hostesses in New York began to serve broccoli, they felt they had made an exciting new discovery. Yet old books about Charleston show that broccoli was eaten there one hundred years ago. But it was forgotten in Charleston for generations, and was really brought to New York from Italy. Now South Carolina is astonished to find that broccoli can be grown easily and profitably in the flats around Charleston. It is not so expensive there as it is in New York, and therefore it is often served without any of the stalk. The crinkly tops are cut off and served with butter, all the stalk part being thrown away. This makes a rather more delicate dish than the usual way of serving broccoli.

— *As served at the Villa Margherita*

Asparagus

Asparagus boiled, served with butter sauce and Parmesan cheese grated over all, makes an unusually nice supper dish. We would suggest serving it with sliced Virginia ham and rice croquettes.

— *Mrs. Rhett*

Okra

There is a story that okra is one of the few vegetables brought from Africa, and that the words okra and buckra (meaning white man) are among the very few African words that have been preserved. In the long, slim islands that separate Charleston from the sea there are few white people. Almost the entire population is colored. These Negroes are so out of touch with the world that it is almost impossible to understand their talk. They speak a dialect called "gullah," a broken-down English with a touch of Huguenot French and Africa Negro. It is these colored folk who especially cherish okra in every form. You never see a cabin on the islands which has not its patch of okra nearby.

Northerners do not always like the gelatinous qualities of okra, but in Charleston this is a popular summer dish. The following is a favorite method of preparing this vegetable.

1 quart tender okra
½ tablespoon lemon juice
1 teaspoon salt
Pepper to taste
1 tablespoon butter

Wash the okra well in cold water. Put in a saucepan with one teaspoon of salt in the water and cook for half an hour. Take from the pot, season with pepper and lemon juice. Add the butter and serve hot, as you would string beans or green peas, with the meat course.

Ophir Cooked Pumpkin

Ophir is one of the plantations of South Carolina which was settled before the American Revolution. The house, standing among its live oaks, is a beautiful example of colonial architecture. A place of joyous activity before the Civil War, it descended, like so many southern plantations, into silence, until recently when it again became the scene of activity. It is now used as a hunting lodge by the famous Yeamans Hall Club.

From Miss Virginia Porcher, whose family has always owned Ophir, comes the Ophir way of cooking pumpkin.

This method is similar to the one used for baking Hubbard squash in many northern homes. Cut slices of pumpkin and place them in a baking pan with a very little water in the bottom. Bake them in the oven, which should be moderately hot, until soft. With a spoon remove the soft pumpkin from the rind and mix with butter, salt and sugar to taste. Put into a baking dish and allow to brown nicely in a hot oven.

— *Miss Virginia Porcher,*
St. James, Berkeley

Apple Charlotte as a Vegetable

Line a buttered baking dish, bottom and sides, with very thin slices of bread, buttered and sprinkled with nutmeg. Fill the center with stewed apples, stopping when half full to put a layer of bits of butter and a few gratings of nutmeg. Then continue filling with apples until the dish is full and bake in a moderate oven (350 degrees F.) for about twenty-five minutes.

Put a meringue on top and set into a slow oven (300 degrees F.) for twelve minutes to brown the meringue. Or instead of a meringue, try marshmallows and brown them in the oven. Do not let the marshmallows touch the edge of the baking dish as they are hard to clean off.

The apples may be either sliced or quartered for stewing, and cooked in a syrup made of one cup of water to one cup of sugar. A little lemon juice added to the syrup improves the flavor of the apples.

This is intended as a luncheon or supper dish to be eaten with the meal, not as dessert.

SALADS AND RELISHES

One lovely moonlight night in my Italian courtyard, I gave a party. A great stone rice-mill wheel served as our table. The old church steeple looked out over our gay dresses and black coats. Needless to say, at this supper Charleston food was served. But I ventured to slip in the recipe given below, which I had always found popular at supper parties in New York.

Stuffed Eggs

6 hard-cooked eggs
2 tablespoons sweet pickle juice
1 tablespoon butter
Salt and pepper

Cut the hard-cooked eggs in half lengthwise, take out the yolks, keeping the whites carefully in shape. Mash the yolks, add the butter and pickle juice and season to taste with salt and pepper. Put the yolk mixture back into whites of eggs; set in a buttered pan and bake for fifteen minutes in a slow oven (300 degrees F.) to brown the uneven points of the egg yolks. These stuffed eggs may be eaten warm or cold.

The recipe may be varied in many ways. Indeed, it is most convenient since almost anything spicy may be used. For instance, mayonnaise can be substituted for the butter, and mustard for the sweet pickle juice. A little caviar is also good in the mixture.

The secret of the success of this recipe is that the eggs are baked after they are stuffed.

—*Helen Woodward*

Grapefruit Aspic with Almonds

2 grapefruit
2 ounces chopped blanched almonds
1 package lemon gelatin
1 cup grapefruit juice
¾ cup boiling water
1 tablespoon sugar

Cut the pulp of the grapefruit in dice and drain. Add the chopped almonds to the grapefruit. Dissolve the gelatin and sugar in the boiling water and add the grapefruit juice. When this is cool and beginning to thicken, add the grapefruit and almond mixture. Pour into a mold and put in the refrigerator to harden.

Serve as a salad with mayonnaise dressing or as a dessert with whipped cream. This recipe makes six servings and is a favorite dish for Sunday night supper in Charleston. — *William's Recipe*

Cinnamon Apple Salad

2 cups sugar
1 cup water
1 cup cinnamon drops (candy)
8 medium-sized firm apples

Peel the apples, leaving a little of the peel around the stem, and core. Put the apples in an open pan on top of the stove, pour over them the water, sugar and cinnamon drops. Cook slowly, turning the apples frequently in the syrup, until done. Cool and place on lettuce leaves, filling the centers of the apples with nuts and cream cheese or with cream cheese and mayonnaise.

They are delicious used as baked apples with the middle filled with the jellied juice in which they were cooked.

If you do not wish a deep rose color, use less of the cinnamon drops.

—*Mrs. Cornelius Youmans Reamer*

Tomato Aspic Jelly

Instead of the bright red jelly which one expects from tomatoes, this is pale, almost pink in color. Egg whites are used to clear the liquid and it is strained through cheese cloth, which results in a light color. The flavor is excellent, however, the seasonings being subtly blended.

1 pint stewed tomatoes
1 small onion, finely chopped
$\frac{1}{2}$ cup chopped celery
$\frac{1}{2}$ cup chopped parsley
2 teaspoons sugar
Salt and red pepper to taste
4 whole cloves
4 whole allspice
2 tablespoons gelatin
1 cup cold water
1 egg white

Put the tomatoes, onion, celery, parsley and seasonings into a saucepan and bring slowly to the boiling point. Remove from the fire, allow to stand for half an hour. Then strain. Mix in the gelatin which has been soaked in the cold water and add the slightly beaten egg white. Place on the fire and cook, without stirring, until the egg-white crust breaks. Remove from the fire, strain through cheese cloth and pour into a mold. Let stand in the refrigerator until firm. This makes six servings.

—*Mrs. William A. Hutchinson*

Tomato and Cheese Aspic I

1 small onion, chopped
$\frac{1}{4}$ green pepper, chopped
2 whole cloves
$\frac{1}{4}$ teaspoon salt
$\frac{1}{4}$ teaspoon Worcestershire sauce

1 sprig parsley, chopped
1 teaspoon sugar
Pepper to taste
2 cups stewed tomatoes
1 cream cheese
1½ tablespoons gelatin
¼ cup water

Add the onion, green pepper, parsley and seasonings to the tomatoes and cook together for five minutes. Soak the gelatin in the cold water and dissolve it in the hot liquid. Then add the cream cheese, breaking it up and stirring until it is almost dissolved. Turn the mixture into a mold and let it stand in the refrigerator until firm. Serve on lettuce with mayonnaise dressing. This will serve six.

—*Mrs. Rhett*

Tomato and Cream Cheese Aspic II

1 pint strained tomatoes
2 cakes cream cheese
¼ cup chopped almonds
1 onion, chopped fine
1 celery heart, chopped fine
½ teaspoon salt
1 teaspoon tarragon vinegar
2 tablespoons gelatin
¼ cup milk
1 cup whipped cream

Heat the tomatoes and cream cheese together, stirring to dissolve the cheese partially. Add the chopped almonds, onion, celery, salt and vinegar. Soak the gelatin in the milk and heat it over steam, stirring until the gelatin is dissolved. Add to the first mixture and fold in the whipped cream. Mold in a ring mold and when firm turn out on lettuce leaves. Serve with mayonnaise dressing.

— *William's Recipe*

Tomato and Cheese Aspic III

Still another cream cheese salad is made by William, this time with prepared gelatin.

1 No. 2 can tomatoes
2 cakes cream cheese
1 bunch celery, chopped fine
1 onion, chopped fine
½ green pepper, chopped fine
Few drops Tabasco sauce
¼ teaspoon black pepper
Salt to taste
2 teaspoons tarragon vinegar
1 package prepared lemon gelatin

Cook the tomatoes for fifteen minutes and strain. Add the celery, onion, green pepper and seasonings and the cream cheese. Stir until the cheese is dissolved. Pour the hot liquid over the prepared gelatin and stir until the gelatin is dissolved. When the mixture has cooled, turn it into a mold and let it harden. When firm, turn out on lettuce leaves and serve with mayonnaise dressing.

— ***William's Recipe***

Cream Cheese Salad

William's cream cheese salads are delicious, but they are very rich and the portions served should be small.

2 cakes cream cheese
1 cup thin cream
¼ cup chopped almonds
½ teaspoon salt
1 teaspoon tarragon vinegar
1 cup whipped cream
2 tablespoons gelatin
¼ cup milk

Warm the thin cream and dissolve the cream cheese in it. Add the chopped almonds, salt and vinegar. Soak the gelatin in the milk and heat it over the steam, stirring until the gelatin is dissolved. Add to the first mixture and fold in the whipped cream. Mold in a ring mold, and when firm turn out on lettuce leaves. This salad is especially good when fruit salad is heaped in the center of the ring.

— ***William's Recipe***

Philadelphia Cream Cheese Salad

2 tablespoons gelatin
½ cup cold water
1 cup boiling water
1 Philadelphia cream cheese
½ green pepper, chopped
1 pimento, chopped
½ cup chopped almonds
½ teaspoon salt
¼ teaspoon paprika
½ cup cream

This is an ideal salad for Sunday night supper. Soak the gelatin in the cold water, dissolve in the boiling water, and allow to cool. Mix the cream cheese, chopped green pepper and pimento and the almonds. Whip the cream. Mix all together with the gelatin and seasonings, adding more salt if desired and fold in the whipped cream last of all. Pour into a mold which has been rinsed with cold water and let stand in the refrigerator until firm. Slice and serve on lettuce with mayonnaise. This makes eight servings.

The salad is white, with the green pepper and pimento giving a decorative bit of color. It is so very rich, however, that we feel that it could well be molded in the very small muffin pans and used chiefly for garnishing, since only tiny portions should be served. About twelve of these portions could be obtained from the recipe.

— *William's Recipe*

Asparagus Salad

Delicious as this salad is when made with canned asparagus, we feel that it would be even better if the fresh vegetable were used.

1 can asparagus tips
2 tablespoons butter
2 tablespoons flour
1 tablespoon gelatin
2 tablespoons cold water
4 egg yolks
Juice of 1 lemon
1 cup cream, whipped
Salt and pepper

Make a sauce of the butter, flour and liquid drained from the asparagus. (There should be one cup of the liquid. Add enough water to make up the amount if there is not one cupful in the can.) Pour the sauce over the beaten egg yolks, return to the fire and cook one minute, stirring constantly. Soak the gelatin in the cold water and add to the hot sauce, stirring until the gelatin is dissolved. When the mixture is cool, add the lemon juice, whipped cream and salt and pepper to taste. Line a mold with a layer of asparagus, pour over half of the sauce, then add another layer of asparagus and the rest of the sauce. This will serve eight. Garnish with mayonnaise and strips of pimento.

—*Mrs. F. S. Munsell, Columbia, South Carolina*

Nut Salad

This salad is decidedly kin to our old friend, Waldorf salad. The boiled dressing, however, is very good and gives a somewhat unusual taste to the apple, nut and celery combination.

For the salad use equal parts of celery, apples and nuts, having them chopped coarsely. Walnuts may be used, but pecans give a better flavor.

For the dressing use:

1 teaspoon ground mustard
½ teaspoon salt
1 teaspoon cornstarch
1 teaspoon sugar
2 egg yolks
½ cup vinegar
¼ cup milk

Mix the dry ingredients together thoroughly and beat in the eggs. Then add the vinegar and cook in the upper part of a double boiler until it begins to thicken. Then stir in the milk. Keep stirring until thick, remove from the fire and allow to cool. Mix with the celery, apples and nuts and serve on lettuce. If one cup of each of the chopped ingredients is used, this will serve six.

—*Miss May Salley, Columbia, South Carolina*

Tomato Salad

6 tomatoes
4 hard-cooked eggs
Mayonnaise dressing
Lettuce

Select firm tomatoes, dip in boiling water, drain and slip off the skins. Set in the refrigerator to chill.

Chop the hard-cooked eggs in large pieces and mix with mayonnaise dressing. Hollow out the centers of the tomatoes, fill with the egg stuffing and serve on lettuce, topping each tomato with a spoonful of mayonnaise. —*Helen Rhett Simons*

Royal Salad

1 small head of red cabbage
1 cup shredded pineapple
1 cup chopped blanched almonds
Mayonnaise
Watercress or lettuce

Cut off the top of the cabbage and hollow it out, leaving a shell of the outer leaves. Soak the cabbage in cold salted water for about half an hour. Drain the small pieces well and chop them. There should be about two cups. Mix this with the pineapple and almonds and add enough mayonnaise to moisten. Fill the shell and top with mayonnaise. Arrange on a bed of watercress or lettuce. This serves six.

— *May Salley, Columbia,*
South Carolina

Salmon Salad

1 cup chopped cabbage
Tarragon vinegar
1 cup canned salmon
Mayonnaise

Chop the cabbage fine and marinate in tarragon vinegar with ice until the cabbage is crisp. Add the flaked salmon to the well-drained cabbage and mix with mayonnaise. Serve topped with mayonnaise and garnish with a dash of paprika. Four small servings.

— *Emma Salley, " Pirate House "*

Salad Dressing

" Old " is the note in the margin of the book in which this recipe was originally written, and after tasting this dressing we are very glad that it has been preserved for later use.

3 hard-cooked eggs
¼ teaspoon salt
1 teaspoon mustard
1 tablespoon vinegar
3 tablespoons oil

Separate the yolks and whites of the hard-cooked eggs and mash the yolks. Add the salt and mustard to them and mix well. Then add the oil and vinegar and stir until thoroughly mixed. Cut up the whites of the eggs finely and add to the dressing.

If this is served with lettuce it makes almost an egg salad. The dressing is also delightful with finely chopped cabbage. The recipe makes about one cup of dressing.

—*Mrs. Shackelford*

Fruit Salad Dressing

½ cup mayonnaise
½ cup whipped cream

Blend the whipped cream and mayonnaise just before serving on the fruit salad. This makes a much more delicate dressing than does mayonnaise alone, and one better adapted to serving with the fruit.

— *William's Recipe*

Russian Sandwiches

½ cup chopped tomatoes
½ cup chopped celery
½ cup chopped olives
Salt and pepper to taste
Mayonnaise
1 tablespoon minced onion

Mix the tomatoes, celery, olives and onion together and season to taste with salt and pepper. Add enough mayonnaise to make it smooth enough to spread, and spread between layers of whole wheat bread.

—*Emma Salley*, "*Pirate House*"

Preserved Cranberries

1 pound cranberries
1 pound sugar
1 cup water

Look over and wash the cranberries. Make a syrup of the sugar and water and boil for about ten minutes, skimming well. Then add the cranberries and boil them slowly, till they are quite soft and of a fine color. The directions then say to "put them into jars (warm) and tie them up with brandy paper when cold." Brandy paper being beyond our reach, we turned them into jelly glasses and sealed each glass with paraffin, adding a thin coating as soon as the glass was filled. When the cranberries were cold, another layer of paraffin was added, and each glass turned so that the paraffin ran well up on the sides of the glass to make a perfect seal. This made four glasses of cranberry sauce.

— *Mary Leize Simons*

Brandy Peaches I

Although the Herald-Tribune Institute was unable to test this recipe for prohibition reasons, it is included because it belongs here.

Select uniform-sized peaches, not too ripe. Put them in a glass jar and cover with ripened corn whiskey. Let them steep ten days; then take out of the whiskey, weigh them, and to each pound of peaches add three-quarters of a pound of white sugar. Let the peaches soak in the sugar until saturated. Then put all in a kettle with a few cloves and spice and boil for half an hour. Pack in jars.

Brandy Peaches II

The Institute has a recipe of its own for brandied peaches, however, which is very good. The peaches, in this case, are forced to manufacture their own brandy! If the spiced flavor characteristic of the Charleston peaches is desired, we suggest adding a very little spice to the sugar and mixing it in well before putting it over the peaches.

Take firm, unblemished peaches, peel and place them in layers in a jar. A bean pot with a loosely fitted cover is the most convenient receptacle to use, but a half-gallon glass jar with screw or clamp top may be used. Cover each layer of peaches with granulated sugar, trying to fill all the crevices between the peaches. When the jar is full, cover it to keep out dust and let it stand until the next day. Open it and you will find that the peaches have shrunk to about half their former size.

Add more peaches and sugar to refill the jar. Keep this up for a week until, after standing over night, the jar remains full. Cover, but do not seal for about six weeks. At the end of that time it is safe to seal the jar. Paraffin may be utilized if a bean pot is used. Let it stand (some housewives bury the jar for six months) for from six to eight months for the best results.

Brandy Peaches III

Another method of brandying peaches which has fallen into disuse is given below. The reason for its disfavor is to be found in the last line.

Scald the peaches in hot water, then dip them in

strong lye, rub them with a coarse cloth and throw them into cold water. Make a syrup of three-quarters of a pound of sugar to one pound of fruit, and when cold put in an equal amount of brandy.

— *Mary Leize Simons*

Pickled Cabbage

Cabbage is a frequent constituent of pickles, but this is the first time we have had it pickled alone. This makes a very sharp pickle — almost a condiment that might be used in place of horseradish. It is very good in an oyster cocktail sauce and may be used sparingly as a relish for meats.

1 large cabbage
$\frac{1}{2}$ cup salt
White wine vinegar
Cloves, mace and allspice

Slice or shred the cabbage very fine. Put it into an earthen dish and sprinkle with the salt, mixing it in well. Cover with another dish and let it stand for twenty-four hours.

Drain the cabbage and take enough vinegar to cover it. Add, for each pint, four whole cloves, two blades mace and four whole allspice. Boil the vinegar for two minutes and pour over the cabbage. Seal in pint jars. This amount makes about three pints.

The directions for sealing are to "cover it close with a cloth. Then tie it over with leather," but we find that the glass jar method is more satisfactory.

—*Bossis*

Green Tomato Pickle I

This green-tomato pickle is a spicy, old-fashioned relish which is particulary good with cold meats. Chopped finely, it may be added to many salads to make an interesting variation.

4 quarts green tomatoes
12 large onions
½ cup salt (about)
¼ cup ground mustard
2 tablespoons black pepper
2 tablespoons ground allspice
1 teaspoon cloves
4 green peppers, chopped fine
1 red pepper, chopped fine
¼ pound white mustard seed
1 pound brown sugar
2 quarts vinegar

Slice the tomatoes and onions very thin. Place in a large dish, sprinkling each layer with a little salt, and let stand twenty-four hours. Drain, put in a kettle and add the other ingredients. Boil down until as thick as catsup. Seal in jars. This makes six pints, and requires about two and three-quarters hours cooking.

—*Mrs. Moore*

Green Tomato Pickle II

One-half the original recipe makes eight pints of pickle and, good as it is, this amount seems sufficient for the average household.

2 quarts green tomatoes
6 large onions
6 green peppers
6 red peppers
1 cup salt
¼ pound green ginger
¼ pound ground mustard
1 ounce allspice
½ ounce cloves
1 ounce ground ginger
¼ pound white mustard seed
½ ounce turmeric
¼ pound grated horseradish
1 nutmeg, grated
¼ cup celery seed
1 cup sugar
3 quarts vinegar
½ ounce mace
½ ounce black pepper

Slice the tomatoes, onions, and peppers and place in an earthen dish in layers. Sprinkle each layer with salt. Let stand for two hours and drain. Add the cut green ginger, sugar, spices and vinegar and cook until thickened — about three hours. Seal in jars. This makes about eight pints.

Red-Pepper Catsup I

This is a very peppery, near-tabasco sauce. A drop or two is all that is needed either directly on meat or in making a sauce. It is very good and most attractive in color, being a bright red.

24 bell peppers
4 onions
1 cup vinegar

Remove the seeds from the peppers, cut them up slightly, add the onions, chopped, and the vinegar and cook until the peppers are soft enough to strain. Put the strained sauce into very small bottles and seal. This makes about one pint of catsup.

— *Mrs. Bennett*

Red Pepper Catsup II

This very peppery relish is more like tabasco sauce than our usual tomato catsups.

3 quarts long red peppers
3 quarts onions
4 quarts vinegar
Salt to taste

Cut up the peppers, removing the seeds. Peel and slice the onions. Cook the peppers and onions in the vinegar until they are soft enough to pass through a meat chopper or until they can be strained. If they are chopped the pieces of pulp will, of course, be larger than if they are strained. Add salt to taste and store in small bottles. This may be served with meat or fish or added to savory sauces.

—*Mrs. E. H. Prioleau*

Pumpkin Chips I

I do not know whether anybody in the North ever makes preserves of pumpkins. I certainly have never seen them. Yet, pumpkin chip is as delicious a conserve as I have ever eaten. It has a sharp lemon flavor.

Peel and slice pumpkin in small chips about one and a half inches by one inch and one-sixteenth of an inch thick. To each pound of chips add a pound of granulated sugar, the juice of two large lemons and the grated rind of half a lemon.

Boil all together until the chips have become transparent. Take out the chips and put into jars.

Continue to boil the stiff syrup until it is thick; then pour it over the chips in the jars.

This is the simplest form of conserve. There are many variations which make pumpkin chips much more delicious. Very small seeded raisins may be added. Also a little green ginger and red pepper. The best pumpkin chips contain all of these ingredients.

Pumpkin Chips II

2 pounds chipped pumpkin
2 pounds sugar
1 dozen lemons

Cut slices from a pumpkin into chips about the size of a half dollar. Wash them, dry them thoroughly, and weigh out two pounds. Add the juice of the lemons, grating the rinds of two before squeezing them. Mix the pumpkin, lemon juice and sugar and boil until the pumpkin is tender, skimming when necessary. When the chips are tender, take them out and boil the syrup again until it is very thick — about two hours in all is required for the cooking. Return the chips to the syrup for a few minutes, adding the grated lemon rind. Seal in jars or turn into jelly glasses and seal with paraffin. This recipe makes two pints.

— *Mrs. Robert B. Lyons*

BREADS

In the North man may not be able to live by bread alone; but in the South, and particularly in Charleston, he comes mighty near to it, provided the bread is hot.

My only regret in giving you these oldtime Charleston recipes for hot breads, for waffles, spoon bread, pop-overs and muffins is that we can't at the same time offer some of that less easily defined charm that belongs to the old town.

Most of the recipes in this chapter come from Miss Elizabeth Harleston's old notebook, which means that these breads have been eaten by a long procession of hungry people from 1800 to the present day. Miss Harleston left her notebook to her niece, in 1887, and she in turn bequeathed it to her daughter, Elizabeth Harleston Fraser, Mrs. Theodore J. Simons, Sr., who now owns it. Through her courtesy we were given the privilege of copying these old pages. These recipes are bound up not only in a long family history, but in the spectacular story of the state of South Carolina.

Rice Griddle Cakes

Rice flour may be used in place of the Indian meal suggested. These cakes are good for breakfast but they may also be served with butter and shaved maple sugar as dessert.

1 cup uncooked rice
2½ cups milk
⅓ cup cornmeal
3 eggs
1 teaspoon salt.

Cook the well-washed rice in the milk in the top of a double boiler until the rice is quite soft. While it is hot stir in the cornmeal and allow it to cool. When cold add the well-beaten eggs and the salt. Bake in small, thin cakes on a hot, greased griddle.

— *Mary Leize Simons*

Rice-Flour Toddles

Since there was no indication on the recipe as to how the "toddles" were to be cooked, we were forced to do a bit of experimenting before we concluded that the best thing to do was to bake them as griddle cakes. They are good served with butter and jelly or with butter and maple syrup.

1 cup cooked hominy
½ cup rice flour
1 egg
1 teaspoon salt
½ cup milk (about)

Mix the rice flour and salt with the hominy and add the beaten egg which has been combined with the milk. Drop on a well-greased griddle and bake until each side is brown. This makes about twelve small cakes.

Wheat flour, used in place of the rice flour, brings out the taste of the hominy more prominently.

— *Miss C. Blanche Moodie*

Corn Batter Cakes
(Griddle Cakes)

2 cups sifted cornmeal
½ cup wheat flour
2 teaspoons baking powder
½ teaspoon salt
1 tablespoon melted butter
1 tablespoon lard, melted
1 egg
1¼ cups milk (about)

Mix and sift the dry ingredients. Add one cup of milk to the egg and add to the dry ingredients. Then add the melted shortening and enough more milk to make a soft dough. Bake as any griddle cakes. This is excellent served with almost any chicken dish or for breakfast with maple syrup.

— *William's Recipe*

Hominy Waffles

A good many of Charleston's favorite hot breads are made with hominy, as is this old recipe for waffles.

1 cup hominy
2 cups flour
1 teaspoon salt
2 cups milk
1 cup water
2 tablespoons butter, melted

Mix the cooked hominy with the sifted flour and salt. Add the milk and water — all milk may be used — and stir in the melted butter. Bake in a hot waffle iron for about four minutes.

A point to remember in baking hominy waffles is that they do not spread as easily as the regular waffle batter. It is well to put a tablespoon of batter in each division of the waffle mold, with an additional spoonful in the center of the iron.

These waffles are crisp on the outside and moist within. They are very delicious and at the same time very economical waffles. They also go farther, for one of these waffles is as satisfying as two of the usual ones. This recipe makes about twelve waffles.

— *Mary Leize Simons*

Rice Flour Waffles

1 cup hominy
1 egg, well beaten
1 cup rice flour
⅓ cup wheat flour
¼ teaspoon salt
1 cup milk
⅓ cup water
1 tablespoon butter, melted

Beat the cold hominy into the egg until it is smooth. Mix and sift the dry ingredients, mix to a batter with the milk and water. Then add the egg and hominy mixture and last the melted butter.

Bake in a hot waffle iron for a trifle longer than usual — allow about four minutes. These waffles are not the crisp product with which we are familiar. They are crispish on the outside but moist within. The flavor is excellent, and while they may be served in almost any preferred manner, we found them particularly good liberally buttered and served with bacon. This recipe makes about eight waffles.

—*Mary Leize Simons*

Breakfast Rusks

Although the name might lead you to expect something very unusual, Charleston breakfast rusks are really only very delicious muffins.

1½ tablespoons butter
¼ cup sugar
1 egg well beaten
1 cup milk
1¾ cups flour
¼ teaspoon salt
3 teaspoons baking powder

Cream the butter and sugar, add the well-beaten eggs and beat well. Mix and sift the dry ingredients and add to the first mixture alternately with the milk. Turn into well-greased muffin tins and bake in a hot oven (400 degrees F.) for about twenty-five minutes. Makes about nine muffins.

—*Mary Leize Simons*

Cream Muffins

The original recipe reads, " One quart of flour, one quart of sweet milk, four eggs and a small piece of butter, salt, of course. Bake in a hot oven." The result is popovers.

Reducing the quantities so that the revised recipe makes twelve popovers, the following amounts are needed:

1 cup flour
$\frac{1}{4}$ teaspoon salt
1 egg, well beaten
1 cup milk
1 teaspoon butter, melted

Mix and sift the flour and salt. Add the egg and milk and lastly the butter. Beat with a wheel egg beater for two minutes. Pour the batter into very hot iron gem pans which must be generously buttered. Bake in a quick oven (425 degrees F.) for about thirty minutes. This makes twelve popovers.

—*Bossis*

Quick Muffins

2 cups flour
1 tablespoon sugar
3 teaspoons baking powder
$\frac{1}{2}$ teaspoon salt
2 eggs, well beaten
1 cup milk
2 tablespoons butter, melted

Mix and sift the dry ingredients. Add the beaten eggs to the milk and add gradually to the dry ingredients. Then add the butter and turn into well-greased muffin tins. Bake for about thirty minutes in a hot oven (400 degrees F.). This recipe makes twelve muffins.

—*Mary Leize Simons*

Rice Muffins I

2 cups flour
4 teaspoons baking powder
½ teaspoon salt
1 cup cold cooked rice
2 eggs, well beaten
1 cup milk
3 tablespoons melted butter

Mix and sift the dry ingredients. Add the rice, stirring well, and then combine with the milk and eggs which have been mixed together. Lastly stir in the melted butter. Turn into well-greased muffin tins and bake in a quick oven (425 degrees F.) for about twenty-five minutes. This recipe makes twelve muffins.

—*Mary Leize Simons*

Rice Muffins II

½ cup flour
½ cup white cornmeal

½ cup boiled rice
¾ teaspoon soda
2 eggs, separated
¾ to 1 cup sour milk

Sift the flour with the soda and mix with the cornmeal and rice. Add the sour milk and the beaten egg yolks and beat until very light. Then fold in the stiffly beaten egg whites and turn into well-greased muffin pans. Bake in a moderately hot oven (375 degrees F.) about twenty-five minutes. This makes twelve muffins.

—*Miss Harleston's Notebook*

Rice Cakes

1 cup soft boiled rice
½ cup milk
½ cup rice flour

Mix the ingredients together and bake on a well-greased tin as you would drop biscuits. Bake in a quick oven (425 degrees F.) for thirty minutes. This amount makes eight small cakes.

These little cakes should be split and buttered generously, for the butter is needed to make them a success. In baking, the rice on the outsides of the cakes acquires a toasted flavor. While butter is the usual accompaniment, syrup may be used with these cakes, or they may be served with preserves.

—*Mary Leize Simons*

Puff Pops

1 cup flour
¼ teaspoon salt
1 egg, well beaten
1 cup milk

Sift the flour and salt together. Mix the egg and milk together and add to the dry ingredients. Beat for two minutes with a wheel egg beater and put into very hot iron gem pans which have been liberally greased. Bake in a quick oven (425 degrees F.) for about half an hour. This recipe makes twelve.

—*Bossis*

Quick Biscuits

2 cups flour
5 teaspoons baking powder
1 teaspoon salt
¼ cup shortening
1 cup milk

Mix and sift the dry ingredients; rub in the shortening and mix with the milk to a soft, thick dough. Drop by spoonfuls onto a well-greased tin and bake in a quick oven (425 degrees F.) for about fifteen minutes. These are best when made with butter and come out of the oven as thin, crusty biscuits rather than the thicker variety. Twelve biscuits.

—*Mary Leize Simons*

Popovers I

1 cup flour
¼ teaspoon salt
1 egg, well beaten
1 cup milk
1½ tablespoons melted butter

Mix and sift the flour and salt. Add the egg and milk and lastly the butter. Beat for two minutes with a wheel egg beater and put the batter into very hot iron gem pans which must be generously buttered. Bake in a hot oven (425 degrees F.) for about thirty minutes. Makes twelve popovers.

—*Mary Leize Simons*

Popovers II

2 cups flour
1 teaspoon salt
2 eggs, well beaten
2 cups milk

Sift the flour and salt together. Combine the beaten eggs and milk and add gradually to the first mixture. Beat with a rotary egg beater for two minutes and turn into hot, well-buttered muffin pans. Bake in a quick oven (425 degrees F.) for about thirty-five minutes. This will make three dozen small popovers.

—*Coming Tee Plantation,*
Cooper River

Ashley Bread

1 cup rice flour
½ teaspoon salt
1½ teaspoons baking powder
1 egg
1 cup milk
1½ tablespoons melted butter

Mix and sift the dry ingredients. Beat the egg well and add the milk to it. Combine with the first mixture. Then stir in the melted butter and turn into a well-greased, shallow pan. Bake in a moderate oven (350 degrees F.) for forty-five minutes.

This is much like other spoon breads except that it has a characteristic rice flavor. Makes eight large pieces.

—*Panchita Heyward Grimball,*
Wappaoolah Plantation,
Cooper River

Batter Bread

This recipe suggests baking spoon or batter bread in individual ramekins. We selected green ones because of the interesting color in conjunction with the yellow hot bread.

1½ cups cornmeal
1½ cups boiling water
3 eggs
1 tablespoon lard or butter
1½ cups milk
2 teaspoons salt

First beat the boiling water into the meal, then add the eggs, unbeaten, and beat hard. Then add the shortening and lastly the milk and salt. Bake in hot, greased ramekins in a hot oven (400 degrees F.) for thirty minutes and serve at once.

For the average family we suggest using half the amounts called for with two eggs and a bit less milk than three-fourths cup.

—*Mary Heyward*

Corn Bread

"Yeast powder" is the leavening agent to be used in this recipe (as in many of the others), but we have translated it into the more prosaic, though identical, "baking powder."

1 cup white cornmeal
¼ cup wheat flour
1 teaspoon baking powder
½ teaspoon salt
1 egg, well beaten
½ cup milk
1 tablespoon butter, melted

Mix and sift the dry ingredients. Add the milk to the well-beaten egg and combine the mixtures. Add the melted butter and turn into a well-greased baking pan and bake in a quick oven (425 degrees F.) for about twenty-five minutes. Eight large pieces.

— *Mary Leize Simons*

Fried Corn Bread

This is an old Aiken County recipe.

2 cups sifted cornmeal
½ cup wheat flour
2 tablespoons baking powder
1 teaspoon salt
1 egg
1 cup sweet milk (about)

Mix and sift the dry ingredients. Add the milk to the beaten egg and combine with the first mixture. The batter should be rather thick. Drop by spoonfuls into deep hot fat and cook until each puff is a rich brown. The batter may be made into small, thin croquettes if a more regular shape is preferred, but we found the irregular puffs more to our liking.

This fried corn bread may be served plain with butter or it may be considered more of a sweet — rather like a fritter, in fact — and served with butter and syrup or butter and jam. Makes eighteen puffs.

—*Mrs. Cornelius Youmans Reamer*

Owendaw Corn Bread

Hominy gives this bread its distinctive flavor. Like all of the spoon breads, it should be eaten very hot with much butter.

1 cup cooked hominy
2 tablespoons butter
2 eggs
1 cup milk
½ cup cornmeal
½ teaspoon salt

While the hominy is hot, stir in the butter. Beat the eggs until light and add to the hominy, then add the milk and lastly the cornmeal and salt. This makes a very thin batter. Pour it into a deep, buttered pan and bake in a moderately hot oven (375 degrees F.) for about thirty minutes. This will serve six. When baked, it has the appearance of a baked batter pudding, and when rich and well mixed it has almost the delicacy of baked custard.

—*Southern Cook Book*

Old Virginia Spoon Bread

1 cup white cornmeal
1 cup boiling water
1 tablespoon butter
1 teaspoon salt
1 egg, well beaten
1 cup rich milk
1½ teaspoons baking powder

Scald the cornmeal with the boiling water, then stir in the butter, salt and well-beaten egg. Add the baking powder and milk. Turn into a well-buttered pan and bake for forty minutes in a moderately hot oven (375 degrees F.). Serve hot with butter. This is an especially delicious bread, and it is not at all difficult to make. This recipe makes eight large portions.

—*Mrs. Frederick Gardener*

Hominy Bread

1 cup cooked hominy
2 eggs, well beaten

1 tablespoon butter
$\frac{1}{4}$ teaspoon salt
Milk, if necessary

Add the hominy to the well-beaten eggs and stir until smooth. If cold hominy is used, melt the butter, or it may be stirred into the warm hominy. Add the salt. If the mixture does not seem very soft — it must be of the consistency of a not-too-thick cake batter — add a little milk. However, if the hominy is of the usual consistency the eggs will provide enough liquid.

Turn the mixture into a well-greased pan and bake in a moderate oven for about forty-five minutes. This bread is not to be eaten in the fingers, but to be cut and lifted out (or served with a spoon!), buttered, and eaten with a fork.

The baking powder has not been omitted. None is required!

— *Mary Leize Simons*

Sweet Sally Lunn

The original recipe called not only for half a pound of butter but for two cups of cream as well! This made such a rich bread that we felt it could be changed without damaging the recipe and the result would be much better for the silhouette. The recipe given below calls for half of the original amounts and makes sixteen small squares.

1 egg
1 cup sugar
1 cup cream
1 cup flour
1 teaspoon baking powder
½ teaspoon mace

Beat the egg, add the sugar and beat again. Sift the mace and baking powder with the flour and add alternately with the cream to the first mixture. Turn into a well-greased square tin and bake in a moderate oven (350 degrees F.) for about half an hour. The cake — it is so sweet that it really falls into this class — is still quite rich.

—*Mrs. Rhett*

Sally Lunn

A less cake-like Sally Lunn is made as follows:

2 cups flour
½ cup sugar
2 teaspoons baking powder
½ teaspoon salt
2 eggs, separated
¾ cup milk
1 tablespoon butter, melted

Add the sugar to the beaten egg yolks. Mix and sift the dry ingredients and add alternately with the milk to the egg and sugar mixture; then add the melted butter. Beat the egg whites until stiff but not dry, and fold them in. Bake in a well-greased square pan or in muffin pans. For the loaf, allow about forty minutes in a moderate oven. The small tins require only about twenty-five minutes. This recipe makes sixteen squares or twelve muffins.

—Mrs. B. C. Webb

Hoe Cake

1 cup white cornmeal
½ teaspoon salt
1 teaspoon sugar
Milk or water

Mix the cornmeal, salt and sugar and add enough boiling milk or water to make a batter which will not spread when put upon the griddle. Grease the griddle with salt pork; drop the mixture on with large spoon. Each cake should be about half an inch thick. Cook slowly, and when browned, put a bit of butter on top of each cake and turn over. They cannot cook too long, provided they do not burn.

Sometimes the dough is put on in one large cake, and as soon as browned underneath it is turned over upon a freshly greased place. The thin, crisp crust is peeled off with a knife, laid on a hot plate and spread with butter. When another brown crust has formed, the cake is turned again, the crust is removed and buttered, and the process continued until the cake is all browned. These crisp, buttered crusts are served piled together and cut in sections.

— *Southern Cook Book*

Philpy

½ cup rice, cooked
6 tablespoons water
½ cup rice flour
1 egg

Boil the washed rice until soft and tender. When cold rub the rice until it is smooth and add the rice flour and water which have been made into a smooth paste. Beat the egg until light and add to the rice mixture. Bake on a well-buttered shallow, tin plate in a quick oven (425 degrees F.) for about thirty minutes.

If the philpy is baked in a pie pan, cut it into sections like those of a pie when serving. It must be very hot and split and buttered at once to be at its best.

— *Carolina Housewife*

Cheese Straws I

1 cup flour
1 cup grated cheese

¼ cup butter
1 egg
½ teaspoon salt
¼ teaspoon red pepper

Mix together the flour, cheese, salt and pepper. Cut in the butter as for pastry and add the beaten egg. If more liquid is needed, add a few drops of water. This should be like pastry. Roll thin, cut in strips and bake in a quick oven (425 degrees F.) until lightly browned. This makes about five dozen straws. — *Mary Leize Simons*

Cheese Straws II

1 cup grated cheese
1 cup flour
¼ teaspoon baking powder
¼ teaspoon salt
¼ teaspoon red pepper
⅓ cup cooking oil
Water

Sift the flour with the baking powder, salt and pepper. Mix with the cheese and add the cooking oil, mixing with a fork. Add water if necessary to make a dough which can be rolled out. Roll to about one-fourth inch in thickness and cut into long narrow strips. Bake in a quick oven (425 degrees F.) until brown, about twenty minutes.

— *Miss Harleston's Notebook*

Light Bread Batter Bread

This recipe offers an opportunity for using up bread crumbs. Mrs. Gardener, who gave us the recipe, writes: "We always called the light bread batter bread by its initials, 'L. B. B. B.,' and we children would see which could say it the fastest."

2 eggs
1 quart milk
1 quart bread crumbs
$\frac{1}{4}$ cup melted butter

Beat the eggs, add the milk and melted butter. Add to the bread crumbs and pour into a buttered pan. Bake for three-quarters of an hour in a hot oven (400 degrees F.). Serve with butter at once, as it falls if allowed to stand when taken from the oven.

—*Mrs. Frederick Gardener*

Yeast Cakes

Most of us would consider that we were hardly used if we had to make our own bread, but if we had first to prepare the yeast to raise the bread — !

This recipe requires, first of all, two yeast cakes (and very different-looking ones from those we are accustomed to) which must be left over from the last yeast-making.

Take two cakes, dissolve in cold water, and with a pint of flour make a stiff batter. Set to rise overnight. In the morning add a pint of cornmeal, and again set to rise. When it is risen add enough meal to make a dough stiff enough to roll out and cut. Put upon a large flat dish to dry, turn every day until dry, then put into a tin box.

—*Anne H. Lyons*

CAKES AND CANDIES

JUST as the eighteenth century passed on its ruffled way Miss Elizabeth Harleston was born on Bossis Plantation. For nearly ninety years (from the time of John Adams to the time of Grover Cleveland) she lived there: and for five generations she was a famous matriarchal hostess. From her columned porch she looked through the moss-hung trees on to Cooper River, meandering lazily on its way to Charleston. Visitors arrived in boats from the river and on horses by land. Negroes moved about, languid of motion but eager of words; and every Negro and every guest knew that Bossis was famous for its cooking. Miss Elizabeth knew it better than anyone, and many an hour she spent writing in her book of recipes.

The material for that notebook began to grow when Nicholas Harleston built the first Bossis Plantation house in 1736. For a century before Miss Elizabeth was born, Bossis was famous for its hospitality. And Miss Elizabeth turned that fame into a culinary glory. There was no strain of Huguenot at Harleston. The cakes in her notebook had no French touch.

With generous hospitality her great niece, Mrs. Simons, brings the ancient enchantment into modern northern kitchens by allowing us to copy some of her best recipes from the old-fashioned pointed handwriting of Miss Elizabeth.

This fruit cake, prepared for her battalions of visitors, is too large for most households today. It can be halved or quartered.

Fruit Cake I

1 pound butter
1 pound sugar
12 eggs
1 pound flour
¾ cup brandy or cooking sherry
¾ cup rosewater
½ ounce cinnamon
1 nutmeg grated
½ teaspoon cloves
Grated rind of one orange
2 pounds seeded raisins
2 pounds currants
1 pound citron cut small

Cream the butter and sugar well together and stir in the twelve eggs, which have been well beaten. Add enough of the flour to the fruit to cover it well and sift the cinnamon, nutmeg and cloves with the remainder of the flour. Add this alternately with the liquids to the first mixture. Then stir in the grated orange rind, and, lastly, the floured fruits.

Grease a large pan well, line it with brown paper and grease the paper. Pour in the cake batter and bake in a slow oven (300 degrees F.) for about four hours. This will make about ten pounds of fruit cake.

The recipe naïvely remarks: "Three times this amount makes a large cake." We agree.

—*Miss Harleston's Notebook*

Fruit Cake II

This recipe is one from the old Ophir Plantation, now a hunting lodge for the Yeaman's Hall Club.

1 pound butter
1 pound sugar
12 eggs
1 cup molasses
1 cup wine or brandy
1 cup rosewater
1 pound flour
$\frac{1}{4}$ pound crystallized orange peel
2 pounds currants

2 pounds raisins
2 pounds citron
1 pound almonds
1 tablespoon grated nutmeg

Cream the butter, adding the sugar a little at a time. Add the eggs one by one, beating well. Add all the liquids and then the fruit mixed with the flour to which the nutmeg has been added. Put in a deep pan, greased and lined with brown paper which should be greased also. Bake the cake three hours in a very slow oven (250 degrees F.) or steam it first and then bake. This makes about twelve and a half pounds of rich fruit cake which is quite dark in color and very full of fruit.

—*Ophir Plantation, St. John's, Berkeley*

White Fruit Cake

2 pounds butter
2 pounds sugar
12 eggs
2 pounds flour
2 ounces nutmeg
2 ounces mace
1 pint brandy or cooking sherry
2 ounces rose water ($\frac{1}{4}$ cup)
3 pounds white raisins
3 pounds cocoanut
3 pounds citron, chopped
3 pounds almonds, chopped

Flour the fruit the day before baking. Cream the butter, add the sugar gradually and when thoroughly blended add the well-beaten eggs. Beat well and add the dry ingredients mixed and sifted together and the liquids. Last of all stir in the floured fruit. The fruit must be well mixed through the cake. Line a large greased baking pan with brown paper, and grease the paper. Turn the cake mixture in and bake in a slow oven (250 degrees F.) for about three hours. This makes a light-colored fruit cake which weighs between eighteen and nineteen pounds.

Quantities of this famous white fruit cake were made by Martha Patterson's mother and given to friends at Christmas time. She usually iced the fruit cake with an almond icing. The icing requires:

1 pound confectioners' sugar
2 egg whites, beaten stiff
Juice of 1 lemon
Orange or rose extract to taste
1 pound almonds, ground fine

Add the sugar and lemon juice to the stiffly beaten egg whites and flavor to taste with the extract. Then add the almonds, ground fine, and spread on the cake.

—*Martha Laurens Patterson*

Cocoanut Fruit Cake

This fruit cake, a dark sun-tan in color, has a particularly flavorful blending of fruits and cocoanut.

1 pound butter
1 pound sugar
12 eggs
1 pound flour
$\frac{3}{4}$ teaspoon cloves
1 teaspoon nutmeg
2 teaspoons cinnamon
1 teaspoon mace
1 cup sherry flavoring
$\frac{1}{2}$ cup rosewater
1 pound raisins
1 pound currants
1 pound citron
1 pound figs
2 pounds almonds
$4\frac{1}{2}$ cups cocoanut

Cream together the butter and sugar very thoroughly and add the well-beaten eggs. Mix and sift the dry ingredients, reserving enough flour to coat the fruit and nuts. Then add the sherry and rosewater alternately with the flour mixture and, last of all, the floured fruit and nuts and the cocoanut. Turn into a large pan which has been greased, lined with several thicknesses of brown paper and greased again. Bake in a slow oven (250 degrees F.) for about three and a half hours. This makes about twelve and a half pounds of fruit cake.

—*Mrs. Haskell*

Lady Baltimore Cake I

Each year at Christmas time hundreds of white boxes go out of Charleston to all parts of the country bearing the round, the tall, the light, the fragile, the ineffable Lady Baltimore cakes. There are several ladies of old descent who make an excellent living baking these famous cakes. You have seen Lady Baltimore cakes on many a menu, but it usually means something altogether different from the real Charleston delicacy.

By no stretch of the imagination could this cake be called economical, but its goodness makes one willing to forget its eight eggs! Half of the cake, however, will make three medium-sized layers.

1 cup butter
2 cups sugar
4 cups flour
4 teaspoons baking powder
1 cup milk

1 teaspoon almond extract
8 eggs, separated

Cream the butter and sugar, add the beaten egg yolks and beat well. Mix and sift the dry ingredients and add alternately with the milk to the first mixture. Flavor with almond extract and last of all add the stiffly beaten egg whites. Turn into well-greased layer cake pans and bake in a moderately hot oven (375 degrees F.) for about twenty-five minutes.

The lemon filling requires

3 cups sugar
½ cup lemon juice
¼ cup boiling water
4 egg whites
2 cups chopped walnuts
2 cups seeded raisins
1 teaspoon vanilla

Add the lemon juice and water to the sugar and cook until it spins a long thread, or to 246 degrees F. Pour the hot syrup over the stiffly beaten egg whites, beating constantly, and continue beating until cold and stiff enough to hold its shape. Flavor with vanilla and add the chopped nuts and raisins. Spread between layers of cake and on top and sides.

Lady Baltimore Cake II

It was this recipe which was used at the Woman's Exchange when Owen Wister wrote *Lady Baltimore.*

½ cup butter
1½ cups sugar
2 eggs, separated
1 cup milk
2 cups flour
1 teaspoon baking powder
½ teaspoon salt

Cream the butter and sugar, add the beaten egg yolks and beat well. Mix and sift the flour and baking powder twice, then sift slowly into the first mixture, adding the milk gradually. Fold in the beaten egg whites last of all. Bake in three well-buttered layer cake pans in a moderately hot oven (375 degrees F.) for about twenty-five minutes.

When the layers are baked, pour the soft filling given below on each layer before you put on the hard filling. It is this filling with the indefinite flavor which makes this cake so distinctive.

1 cup sugar
½ cup walnut meats
¼ cup water
1 teaspoon vanilla
1 teaspoon almond extract

Put the sugar, walnut meats and water into a saucepan and cook to the very soft ball stage (234 degrees F.). Remove from the fire and let cool until lukewarm (110 degrees F.). Add the flavorings and beat until slightly thickened before pouring on cake.

For the hard filling use

2 cups sugar
½ cup water
2 egg whites
1 teaspoon vanilla
1 teaspoon almond extract
Juice of ½ lemon
1 cup chopped raisins
1 cup chopped walnuts

Bring the sugar and water to the boiling point and cook until it will form a firm ball (246 degrees F.). Pour slowly over the stiffly beaten egg whites, beating constantly, and continue beating until cool, adding the raisins, nuts, flavoring and lemon juice as it begins to harden.

—*Alicia Rhett Mayberry*

Lady Baltimore Cake III

This is a very good cake, though it lacks the subtly flavored filling which makes the Lady Baltimore cake glorified by Owen Wister so distinctive.

½ cup butter
1 cup sugar
4 eggs, separated
½ cup milk
2 cups flour
2 teaspoons baking powder
¼ teaspoon salt
½ teaspoon almond extract

Cream the butter, add the sugar gradually and add the beaten egg yolks. Mix and sift the dry ingredients and add alternately with the milk to the first mixture. Stir in the flavoring and last of all fold in the stiffly beaten egg whites. Turn into well-buttered layer cake pans and bake in a moderately hot oven (375 degrees F.) for about twenty-five minutes. This is one-half the original recipe and makes two large layers.

To frost the two-layer cake use:

1½ cups sugar
⅜ cup boiling water
2 egg whites
¼ teaspoon cream of tartar
¾ teaspoon vanilla
1 cup raisins
1 cup broken walnut meats

Boil the sugar and water together until 246 degrees is reached. Beat the egg whites stiffly and add the cream of tartar. Pour the syrup over them in a thin stream, beating constantly, and continue beating until it is stiff enough to hold its shape. Then add the vanilla, raisins and walnuts and spread between the layers and on the top of the cake.

— *Southern Cook Book*

Wedding Cake

One of the most famous of the plantations on the Cooper River is called "The Bluff." General Francis Marion, the "Swamp Fox" of the American Revolution, knew the old place well, and many of his letters were found some years ago in the brick walls of an old building on the grounds. On this plantation is one of the oldest ferries in the country, the charter for which was issued in 1704. It is called the Strawberry Ferry, because it lands at the Strawberry Plantation on the other side of the river. In the plantation house at The Bluff there was a room known as "Travelers' Joy," where tired travelers were put up overnight when the weather was too bad to cross the river. Such travelers were always taken in and treated as expected guests.

Many was the wedding conducted through the decades on The Bluff Plantation. And many a mountainous cake was made there and carried elsewhere for other brides, brides in pantalets and brides in hoop skirts and brides in bustles. And now here is the recipe for this famous wedding cake, ready for the brides of today.

The original recipe is very indefinite as to the quantity of flour required for this cake. One pound makes a darker and richer cake than the quantity given below, and it may be used if preferred. However, with the one pound of flour there seems to be an excess amount of butter, and decreasing the butter does not give as satisfactorily flavored a cake. We concluded that a pound and a half of flour was the best amount to use.

1½ pounds butter
1½ pounds sugar
8 eggs
1½ pounds flour
1 tablespoon ground mace
2 nutmegs
1 cup black molasses
½ cup brandy or cooking sherry
1 cup coffee
1 tablespoon rose extract
2 pounds raisins
3 pounds currants
1 pound chopped almonds
1 pound citron, cut fine

Prepare the fruit and nuts and dredge with part of the flour. Cream the butter and sugar together and add the well-beaten eggs. Mix and sift the flour and spices and add to the egg mixture. Add the fruit and liquids by degrees. Line a large baking pan with brown paper, greasing the pan well and then greasing the paper. Turn in the cake mixture and bake in a slow oven (250 degrees F.) for about three hours. This makes a little over twelve pounds of cake.

An almond filling for the wedding cake is suggested, to be made as follows: Blanch almonds and grind through meat chopper. Add egg whites and pulverized sugar and rose water until of right consistency. Cover with boiled icing after placing on top of cake. Almond filling should be one and a half inches in thickness on top of cake. This might be done, of course, but it seems a rather needless gilding of the lily.

— *Miss Charlotte Ball*
(*from The Bluff Plantation*)

Black Cake

Chocolate is added to this fruit cake to make it darker. It is very rich and well deserves the name of "black cake." If more variety is desired in the fruit, preserved cherries and pineapple might be substituted for part of the raisins and a pound of chopped almonds in place of one pound of currants.

1 pound butter
1 pound sugar
11 eggs
1 pound flour
3 nutmegs, grated
2 teaspoons mace
1 teaspoon ground cloves
½ pound sweet chocolate, grated
½ cup rose water
1½ cups brandy or cooking sherry
4 pounds seeded raisins
4 pounds currants
2 pounds citron, chopped fine

Cream the butter and sugar and add the eleven eggs, well beaten. Dredge the prepared fruit with part of the flour and sift the rest with the spices. Add the flour and liquids alternately to the first mixture and last of all stir in the fruit. Place in a large pan which has been greased, lined with brown paper, and greased again. Bake about three and a half hours in a slow oven (250 degrees F.). This makes about fifteen pounds of fruit cake.

—*Mary Leize Simons*

Chocolate Cake

This makes a very large chocolate layer cake which seemed, to our taste, a trifle dry. Three-fourths of a cup of milk would seem a better proportion.

- 2/3 cup butter
- 2 cups sugar
- 5 eggs, separated
- 3 cups flour
- 2 teaspoons baking powder
- 1/2 teaspoon salt
- 2/3 cup milk
- 1 1/8 teaspoons vanilla

Cream the butter and sugar and add the well-beaten egg yolks. Mix and sift the dry ingredients and add alternately with the milk to the first mixture. Add the vanilla and fold in the stiffly whipped egg whites. Turn into buttered layer cake pans — this makes three large layers — and bake in a moderately hot oven (375 degrees F.) for about twenty-five minutes. Put together with the chocolate icing given below.

- 5 squares chocolate, grated
- 1 1/2 cups sugar
- 1/2 cup water
- 1 teaspoon vanilla

Boil the chocolate, sugar and water together until the very soft ball stage (234 degrees F.) is reached. Remove from the fire, add the vanilla, but do not stir. Let stand until lukewarm (110 degrees F.) and then beat until of the consistency to spread on the cake.

—*Bossis*

Scripture Cake

Fortunately for most of us, this scripture cake recipe is translated into more prosaic language than " 1 tablespoon Judges 14: 8."

1 tablespoon honey
1 cup butter
2 cups sugar
6 eggs
1 cup water
3½ cups flour
2 teaspoons baking powder
½ teaspoon salt
1 teaspoon cinnamon
¾ teaspoon mace
¾ teaspoon nutmeg
½ teaspoon cloves
1 cup chopped almonds
1 cup chopped figs
2 cups raisins
1 teaspoon almond extract

Cream the butter and sugar, add the egg yolks and beat well. Add the honey and then alternately the mixed and sifted dry ingredients and the water. Then add the almonds, figs and raisins, the almond extract and last of all the stiffly beaten egg whites. Turn into a well-greased shallow pan and bake in a moderate oven (350 degrees F.) for about fifty minutes.

— *Miss Emmie Bellinger*

White Cake

½ cup butter
1 cup sugar
1½ cups flour
1 teaspoon baking powder
⅛ teaspoon salt
½ cup sweet milk
4 egg whites

Cream the butter and add the sugar gradually. Cream well together. Mix and sift the dry ingredients and add alternately with the milk. Beat the eggs until stiff, but not dry, and fold them in. Half a teaspoon of vanilla may be added before the egg whites are folded in, if a flavoring is desired. Turn into a loaf pan — this cake is especially nice baked in a square tin — and bake in a moderate oven (350 degrees F.) for about forty minutes.

This cake is of a good texture, rather rich, but most delicious. Its keeping qualities are excellent, for at the end of a week it was still quite moist, while two or three days after making it seemed better than when fresh.

— *Mary Leize Simons*

Marble Cake

This marble cake is very unusual — a combination of lemon cream and spice cake — and the recipe makes a very large cake. However, it keeps moist for some time after making and we have yet to hear any objections to our making the whole amount.

For the white part of the cake use:

½ cup butter
1½ cups sugar
1 cup sour cream
2½ cups flour
½ teaspoon soda
½ teaspoon cream of tartar
2 teaspoons lemon extract
4 egg whites

Cream the butter and sugar well together. Mix and sift the dry ingredients and add to the first mixture alternately with the sour cream. Flavor with the lemon extract and fold in the stiffly beaten egg whites.

For the brown cake use:

½ cup butter
½ cup brown sugar
4 egg yolks
1 cup molasses
½ cup sour cream
2½ cups flour
½ teaspoon soda
½ teaspoon cream of tartar
½ teaspoon cinnamon
¼ teaspoon each mace, nutmeg and cloves

Cream the butter and sugar, add the beaten egg yolks and beat well. Add the molasses. Mix and sift the dry ingredients and add to the first mixture alternately with the cream.

Bake in layers, putting first a spoonful of light and then of dark batter in the pan. About half an hour in a moderately hot oven (375 degrees F.) will be required for baking. This cake may also be baked in a shallow loaf if preferred. It will, of course, require a longer time for baking.

— *Mary Leize Simons*

Orange Cake

Although there is no orange tinge to either the cake or the icing, the flavor of both is distinctly orange. The cake itself seems a bit dry to our taste and we suggest modifying the recipe as given below by adding one-half cup of orange juice in place of the one-quarter cup called for.

1 cup butter
2 cups sugar
5 egg yolks
2 egg whites
3¼ cups flour
¼ teaspoon salt
3 teaspoons baking powder
Grated rind of 2 oranges
¼ cup orange juice
¾ cup milk

Cream the butter, add the sugar gradually and then the eggs well beaten and the grated orange rind. Stir well together. Mix and sift the dry ingredients and add alternately with the milk and orange juice to the first mixture. Turn into well-greased layer cake pans and bake in a moderately hot oven (375 degrees F.) for about twenty-five minutes. This makes three large layers.

For the frosting use:

1 pound granulated sugar
⅓ cup orange juice
3 egg whites

Make a boiled frosting by cooking the sugar and orange juice until 246 degrees F. is reached.

Pour the syrup gradually onto the stiffly beaten egg whites, beating constantly, and continue beating until stiff enough to spread.

An uncooked frosting may be made instead by mixing the orange juice with one pound of confectioners' sugar and folding this into the stiffly beaten egg whites.

— *Miss Mitchell*

Lemon Cake

This is a very delicious cake. The original recipe calls for eight eggs, but since one half of this will make three layers we are using that amount. The cake itself is moist and well-flavored while the lemon filling is just tart enough to be perfect in combination with a butter icing.

¾ cup butter
1½ cups sugar
4 eggs, separated
1 teaspoon lemon extract
¾ cup milk
2½ cups flour
1½ teaspoons baking powder
¼ teaspoon salt

Cream the butter and sugar thoroughly and add the egg yolks well beaten. Stir in the flavoring and add the dry ingredients mixed and sifted together alternately with the milk. Then fold in the stiffly beaten egg whites. Bake in well-buttered layer cake pans in a moderately hot oven (375 degrees F.) for about twenty-five minutes.

For the filling use:

1 cup sugar
3 tablespoons cornstarch
1 cup boiling water
2 eggs
Juice of 2 large lemons
2 tablespoons butter

Mix the sugar and cornstarch well together and add the boiling water gradually. Beat the eggs, mix with the first mixture slowly and add the lemon juice and butter. Cook, stirring constantly, until it thickens. This takes about five minutes. Spread between the layers of the cake and cover the top and sides with a butter frosting.

Silver Cake

For the cake use:

½ cup butter
1½ cups sugar
2½ cups flour
2 teaspoons baking powder
¼ teaspoon salt

1½ cups milk
4 egg whites

Cream the butter and sugar well together. Mix and sift the dry ingredients and add alternately with the milk to the first mixture. Then add the stiffly beaten egg whites, folding in carefully. Turn into well-greased layer cake pans and bake about twenty-five minutes in a moderately hot oven (375 degrees F.). Use the following filling between the layers and over the outside of the cake:

1 cup sugar
½ cup water
2 egg yolks
Juice of 2 lemons
¼ teaspoon vanilla
1 cup walnuts or pecans
½ cup almonds
1 cup raisins

Boil the sugar and water together without stirring after the sugar is dissolved until it spins a thread, or to 242 degrees F. Pour the syrup over the yolks of the eggs, beating constantly, and continue beating until cold. Add the lemon juice and vanilla. Then add the chopped nuts and the raisins.

The nuts and raisins may be soaked overnight in sherry wine flavoring and the almonds sprinkled over the icing instead of mixing them in with the other ingredients.

The icing is a pale yellow in color and rather soft. The flavor is decidedly lemony and blends well with the cake.

—*Mrs. Emma Tabor Waring,*
Fort Motte

Lemon Cocoanut Mountain

⅔ cup butter
2 cups sugar
5 eggs, separated
⅔ cup milk
3 cups flour
1 teaspoon soda
2 teaspoons cream of tartar
½ teaspoon salt

Cream the butter and sugar together thoroughly and add the well-beaten egg yolks. Mix and sift the dry ingredients and add alternately with the milk. Then fold in the stiffly beaten egg whites. Although the recipe does not call for any flavoring, we felt that the addition of a teaspoon of vanilla was an improvement. Turn into layer cake pans which have been well buttered and bake in a moderately hot oven — 375 degrees — for about twenty minutes. This makes three large layers.

For the filling use

2 egg whites
1½ cups powdered sugar
1½ cups cocoanut
Grated lemon rind

Beat the eggs until stiff, add the powdered sugar and the grated cocoanut. Spread between the layers of cake, which should have been allowed to cool, and sprinkle the top liberally with powdered sugar.

—*Mary Leize Simons*

Cocoanut Cream Cake

William's recipe reads: "Make three layers of plain cake. When cooked and cooled squeeze two juicy oranges between layers. Cover with whipped cream. Sprinkle with cocoanut. Cover top of cake with cocoanut mixed with whipped cream. This will make a delicious cocoanut cake."

A more standardized version would be:

3 layers of cake
1½ cups grated cocoanut
2 oranges
1 pint of cream
2 egg whites

Spread two layers of the cake with the juice and pulp of the oranges. Whip the cream with the egg whites and divide it into three parts. Put one-third over each of the two layers and sprinkle each of the two layers with one-half cup cocoanut. Then mix the remaining half cup of cocoanut with the whipped cream and cover the top of the cake with it.

No-Name Cake

While this cake is apparently nameless, that in no way interferes with its goodness either as a layer or loaf cake.

1 cup and 1 tablespoon butter
2 cups very fine sugar
5 eggs, separated
3 cups flour
2 teaspoons of baking powder
1 cup milk
1½ teaspoons vanilla

Cream together the butter and sugar. (Confectioners' sugar was suggested for this cake, but since this tends to make a dry cake we sifted our granulated sugar through a very fine sieve instead and still had a delicate cake.) Add the beaten egg yolks and beat well. Mix and sift the dry ingredients and add alternately with the milk to the first mixture. Add the vanilla and last of all fold in the stiffly beaten egg whites. Bake in layer cake pans in a moderately hot oven (375 degrees F.) for about twenty-five minutes or bake in a large shallow loaf pan for about forty-five minutes in a moderate oven (350 degrees F.).

— *Mary Leize Simons*

1-2-3-and-4 Cake

"One of butter, two of sugar, three of flour and four eggs" seems to be the foundation of a good cake in all parts of the country.

1 cup butter
2 cups sugar
4 eggs, separated
3 cups flour
3 teaspoons baking powder
½ teaspoon salt
1 cup milk
1½ teaspoons vanilla

Cream the butter and sugar, add the well-beaten egg yolks and mix well. Sift the dry ingredients together and add alternately with the milk to the first mixture. Flavor with the vanilla and fold in the stiffly beaten egg whites. Turn into well-greased layer cake pans and bake about thirty minutes in a moderately hot oven (375 degrees F.). Or for a loaf cake bake in a tube cake pan for about fifty minutes in a moderate oven (350 degrees F.).

—*Bossis*

Croton Sponge Cake

Just why the name we do not know, for this cake belongs to the butter cake classification. It is an excellent layer cake, however, and half the recipe makes two good-sized layers.

1 cup butter
2 cups sugar
6 eggs, separated
4 cups flour
1 teaspoon soda
2 teaspoons cream of tartar
1 cup milk

Rub the butter and sugar to a cream, beat the eggs separately. Mix and sift the dry ingredients (the original directions say to add the soda to the milk, but there is no advantage in this procedure) and add them alternately with the milk to the butter-sugar-egg yolk mixture. Vanilla and lemon extract may be added, although the recipe does not call for flavoring. Last of all fold in the stiffly beaten egg whites. Turn into well-greased layer cake pans and bake for twenty minutes in a moderately hot oven (375 degrees F.).

A lemon butter filling between the layers and boiled icing over the outside makes a cake fit for the most special occasion!

—*Mrs. A. H. Lyons*

Washington's Prune Cake

My cook Washington called this a small cake, but The Herald Tribune Institute did not find it so. It filled the usual square loaf pan which Miss Gay uses for the average size cake. The juice which clings to the prunes furnishes the only liquid in the cake except for the eggs. If more moisture is needed, add a little of the prune juice. Unless the prunes are very sweet, it would be wise to add a little sugar to them during the cooking.

2 eggs
3 tablespoons butter, melted
1 cup sugar
1 teaspoon vanilla
2 cups flour
2 teaspoons baking powder
½ teaspoon salt
¾ pound prunes, well cooked

Beat the eggs, then add the melted butter, sugar and vanilla. Stir well and add the flour sifted with the salt and baking powder. Cut the prunes up fine, removing the stones, and mix them in. Stir well, turn into a buttered cake pan and bake in a moderately hot oven (375 degrees F.) for about one hour. This makes a cake which is somewhat reminiscent of apple sauce cake.

— *Washington's Recipe*

Golden Cake

½ cup butter
1 cup sugar
4 egg yolks
1½ cups flour
1 teaspoon baking powder
⅛ teaspoon salt
½ cup sweet milk

Cream the butter, add the sugar gradually and cream well together. Add the well-beaten egg yolks and stir thoroughly. Mix and sift the dry ingredients and add alternately with the milk. Half a teaspoon of vanilla may be added if a flavoring is desired. Turn into a loaf pan — this cake is especially nice baked in a square tin — and bake in a moderate oven (350 degrees F.) for about forty minutes.

This cake is of a good texture, rather rich but most delicious. Its keeping qualities are excellent and it seems to improve with age, up to a certain point, at least. At the end of a week it was still quite moist, while three days after making it seemed much better than when fresh.

— *Mary Leize Simons*

Spice Cake

The mace gives this spice cake a somewhat unusual flavor. It is moist and keeps well — under lock and key.

$\frac{1}{2}$ cup butter
1 cup sugar
3 eggs
1 cup molasses
$\frac{1}{4}$ cup milk
2 cups flour
1 teaspoon soda
1 teaspoon nutmeg
$\frac{1}{2}$ teaspoon mace
$1\frac{1}{2}$ teaspoons cloves

Cream the butter and sugar together, add the beaten eggs and beat well. Add the molasses and milk and then the mixed and sifted dry ingredients. Bake in a shallow loaf cake pan in a moderately hot oven (375 degrees F.) for about thirty minutes.

This recipe was signed on the original sheet as "Grandma's Own, Birdfield Plantation, South Carolina."

Sponge Cake I

The original recipe reads: "Ten eggs, one pound of sugar, half pound of flour. You may add two ounces of bitter almonds and two ounces of sweet almonds if you like. Flavor according to taste."

We did like the almond flavoring and found that half the recipe makes a medium-sized sponge cake.

5 eggs, separated
1 cup sugar
1 cup flour
1 ounce bitter almonds
1 ounce sweet almonds
½ teaspoon vanilla

Beat the egg yolks until lemon colored. Add the sifted sugar, beating well. Stir in the finely chopped almonds and the vanilla. Then fold in the stiffly beaten egg whites. Sift the flour four times and fold carefully into the first mixture. Turn into an ungreased cake pan and bake in a slow oven (300–325 degrees F.) about forty-five minutes.

—*Mary Leize Simons*

Sponge Cake II

The original recipe reads: "Six eggs. Their weight in sugar, one-half their weight in flour.

Grated rind and juice of 1 lemon. Beat sugar and egg yolks together until very light. Add whites beaten stiff, fold in flour and lemon."

In case scales are not handy, these amounts will be nearly correct if average-sized eggs are used:

6 eggs, separated
1½ cups sugar
1½ cups flour
Grated rind and juice of 1 lemon

Separate the eggs and beat the yolks very light. Add the sugar and beat again. Fold in the stiffly beaten egg whites. Sift the flour and fold it in gradually, add the lemon juice and rind. Bake in unbuttered angel cake pan in a slow oven (300 degrees F.) for about fifty minutes. This makes a large sponge cake.

If it is necessary to use a pan which has been greased, it should be buttered and then floured before the batter is put in.

—*Mary Heyward*

Angel Cake

5 egg whites
⅛ teaspoon salt
1 cup sifted sugar
¾ cup flour
¾ teaspoon cream of tartar
1 teaspoon vanilla

Beat the egg whites with the salt until stiff but not dry. Add the sugar gradually, beating it in well. Mix and sift the flour and cream of tartar together four times and fold in lightly. Add the vanilla and pour into an ungreased angel cake pan. If a pan which has never been greased is not available, butter the pan lightly and flour it. Bake in a moderately slow oven (325 degrees F.) for about forty-five minutes. Makes one small cake.

—*Bossis*

Jelly Cake Rolled Up

3 eggs
1 cup sugar
1 cup flour
1 teaspoon cream of tartar
½ teaspoon soda
1 glass currant jelly

Beat the eggs until very light. Add the sugar and then the dry ingredients which have been mixed and sifted together. Turn into a buttered and floured pan — an oblong one is preferable — having the batter not over one-half inch thick. Bake in a moderate oven (350 degrees F.) for twelve to fifteen minutes.

Have ready a clean towel or cloth and when the cake is done slip it out, bottom side up, on the cloth. If the edges on the long sides have baked too hard, trim them off. Spread the cake quickly with the jelly and, commencing at the end, roll it up, wrapping tightly with the cloth. Let it stand with the cloth around it until cool to help keep it in shape. When ready for use, slices are cut from one end.

—*Mary Leize Simons*

Lemon Butter

Although jelly is traditional for rolled cake, this lemon butter is a Charleston suggestion which almost surpasses the jelly! If you feel, however, that lemon butter would be out of place in a " jelly roll," try it as a cake filling. The amount given will cover two layers.

2 eggs
1 cup sugar
2 tablespoons butter
2 lemons

Beat the eggs and sugar together. Add the butter and then the grated rind and juice of the lemons. Bring to the boiling point and cook until thick, stirring constantly or, better yet, cook in the upper part of a double boiler. Spread on the cake.

—*Miss Mitchell*

Boiled Icing

2 cups sugar
½ cup water
3 egg whites
1 tablespoon lemon juice

Put the sugar and water into a saucepan and stir until the sugar is dissolved. Cover and let boil for two or three minutes. Then remove the cover and boil without stirring until 246 degrees is reached. Have the egg whites stiffly beaten and pour the syrup on them in a thin stream, beating constantly. Continue the beating until the frosting is thick and holds its shape, adding the lemon juice toward the end of the beating.

This makes a very fluffy icing and the lemon juice not only flavors it but increases the whiteness of the frosting.

Filling

1 rule boiled icing
½ cup chopped walnuts
¼ cup candied cherries
¼ cup candied pineapple
½ cup raisins
Selected nuts for top of cake

Reserve part of the icing for the top and sides of the cake. Mix the chopped nuts and fruit with the rest of the icing and spread over the layers. Ice the top and sides of the cake and decorate with halves of walnuts. Sliced cherries may also be used in garnishing.

—*Mrs. F. W. Munsell*

Chocolate Icing

A modern touch is this recipe for chocolate icing. Miss Anita de Saussure tells us it cannot fail.

This icing is not boiled and failure seems to be impossible — certainly a recommendation to any cook! This is sufficient icing for a two-layer cake.

2 cups confectioners' sugar
¼ cup cocoa
¼ cup hot coffee (about)
1 tablespoon butter
1 teaspoon vanilla

Mix the confectioners' sugar and cocoa. Pour the hot coffee over the butter, and when it melts beat this into the dry ingredients, adding the vanilla. When of the right consistency spread on the cake. If the icing seems too stiff, add a little more coffee; if too thin, more sugar.

—*Anita de Saussure*

Marshmallow Filling

The original recipe used powdered white gum arabic, but later marshmallows were substituted.

1 cup sugar
½ cup water
2 egg whites
½ pound marshmallows

Boil the sugar and water together until they will spin a long thread or until 246 degrees F. is reached. Remove from the fire and when the bubbling stops, pour in a thin stream over the stiffly beaten egg whites, beating constantly. When the syrup is all in, add the marshmallows which have been cut fine and beat the filling until stiff and cold.

—*Mrs. Lanier Eason*

Caramel Filling

3 cups brown sugar
1 cup butter
1½ cups cream
8 squares (½ pound) chocolate, grated

Put the ingredients into a large saucepan and cook, stirring constantly, until the sugar is dissolved and the chocolate melted. Let the mixture continue cooking until the temperature is 234 degrees F., or a little of the filling dropped in cold water will form a soft ball. Remove from the fire and beat until thick and creamy — usually until the filling is cool — and it will hold its shape.

This recipe makes enough to ice a large three-layer cake. The filling is, as might be imagined, very rich, but the flavor is marvelous and its keeping qualities — if allowed to remain uneaten long enough for one to test them — are remarkable. At the end of a week, the filling was quite as good as the day it was made. The butter kept it soft and it seemed even more mellow than at first.

— ***Mary Leize Simons***

Peanut Cookies

½ cup butter
1 cup sugar
1 egg
½ cup flour
¼ teaspoon salt
2 cups chopped peanuts

Cream the butter, add the sugar gradually, and beat in the well-beaten egg. Sift the flour and salt together and add with the peanuts. Drop from a spoon on a well-greased cookie sheet and bake in a moderate oven (350 degrees F.) from fifteen to twenty minutes. This makes about four dozen cookies, very rich in peanuts. In fact, the idea is to use just enough other ingredients to make the peanuts stick together!

—*Helen Rhett Simons*

Lady Fingers

4 eggs, separated
3 ounces powdered sugar
3 ounces sifted flour
½ cup rose or orange flower water

Beat the egg whites stiffly. At the same time have the yolks beaten with the powdered sugar. Combine the two and fold in the flour and then the rose or orange flower water. Have ready some cookie sheets (rubbed with white wax, the directions read, but greased will do) and form the cakes with a spoon in lady-finger shape. Sprinkle white sugar over each, let them lie until the sugar melts and they shine. Then put them in a moderate oven (350 degrees F.) until they brown delicately—about seven minutes. When cool, take them from the sheets and lay them together in couples, back to back. They may also be baked round. In this form we made six dozen tiny cakes from this recipe.

—*Mary Leize Simons*

Sweet Wafers

4 ounces butter
4 ounces sugar

3 eggs
1½ teaspoons cinnamon
6 ounces flour

Cream the butter and sugar together thoroughly. Add the eggs, well beaten, and gradually stir in the flour and cinnamon sifted together. Drop on well-greased cookie sheets and bake in a moderate oven (350 degrees F.) for about ten minutes. This will make about three and a half dozen cookies.

—*Miss Harleston's Notebook*
Mary Leize Simons

Macaroons

Bitter almonds give these macaroons their fine flavor.

¾ pound sweet almonds
¾ pound bitter almonds
3 cups sugar
6 egg whites

Blanch the almonds and chop them as fine as possible. Beat the egg whites until they are very stiff and fold in the sugar and then the finely chopped almonds. Drop on buttered paper and bake in a slow oven (300 degrees F.) from fifteen to twenty minutes. This makes about nine dozen macaroons.

—*Mrs. Ball, "Commingtee"*

Alderney Cakes

1 cup butter
1 cup brown sugar
1 cup milk
1 teaspoon soda
1 teaspoon nutmeg
$2\frac{1}{2}$ cups flour
1 cup broken nut meats

Cream the butter and sugar together. Mix and sift the dry ingredients and add alternately with the milk to the first mixture. Spread out in a well-greased, shallow pan and sprinkle with the nut meats. Bake in a quick oven (425 degrees F.) for about fifteen minutes and cut into squares while hot. This makes about two dozen squares.

These cakes may have a little more flour added and then be rolled out as any rolled cookies but this makes them rather more troublesome to make, and the squares with nut meats on are very attractive.

Sugar Biscuits

$\frac{2}{3}$ cup sugar
2 tablespoons butter
1 egg
$1\frac{1}{3}$ cups flour
$\frac{1}{2}$ teaspoon cinnamon

Despite the lack of baking powder and liquid, this recipe is correct! The result is a cinnamon-flavored sugar cookie which compares favorably with more expensive ones.

Cream the butter and sugar, add the egg well beaten and the dry ingredients mixed and sifted together. Roll in waxed paper and place the roll in the ice box to chill for several hours or overnight. When ready to bake, cut in thin slices and lay on a well-greased baking sheet. Bake in a quick oven (425 degrees F.) for about twelve minutes. Makes two dozen cookies.

—*Miss Harleston's Notebook*

Shrewsberry Cakes I

The original recipe, dated 1790, reads: "Three-quarters of a pound of sugar, half pound of butter, four eggs, one pound of flour, a little mace or nutmeg and rosewater. Drop on tin sheets and bake in a slow oven."

A later revision uses the same ingredients but gives the following method: "Sift sugar and nutmeg and mace into flour; add rosewater and eggs beaten light and mix well with the flour. Then pour into it as much melted butter as is needed to make a stiff dough. Roll thin and cut into shapes. Bake quickly."

We suggest:

2 cups sugar
1 teaspoon nutmeg
1 teaspoon mace
4 cups flour
4 teaspoons rosewater
4 eggs
½ cup melted butter (about)

Mix and sift the dry ingredients. Beat the eggs until light and add the rose water. Combine with the first mixture and add as much of the melted butter as is necessary to make a stiff dough. Roll the dough in waxed paper, having the roll about two inches in diameter, and chill overnight in the ice box. Cut into thin slices and bake on buttered cookie sheets in a moderate oven (350 degrees F.) for about twelve minutes. Makes six dozen cakes — cookies, really — with a distinctive flavor.

— *Miss Harleston's Notebook*

Shrewsberry Cakes II

1 pound flour (4⅓ cups)
¾ pound butter (1½ cups)
1 pound sugar (2⅓ cups)
1 egg

Cream the butter and sugar thoroughly and add the flour, mixing the last of it in by kneading on a bread board as for shortbread. Add the egg, not beaten, and knead all together. Roll out as thin as possible and cut out with a cookie cutter. Lift onto well-greased cookie sheets with a broad knife and bake in a brisk oven (425 degrees F.) for about twelve minutes, watching that they do not burn. Makes six dozen cakes very like Scotch shortbread.

—*Mrs. Charles Albert Hill*
(*from Patience Pennington*)

Kiss Cakes

"Beat the whites of twelve eggs," nonchalantly requests this recipe, "stir in a pound of finely sifted loaf sugar, continue beating while you put in the sugar or it will fall, add twenty drops of the essence of lemon. Drop on paper and dry in a warm oven."

Since three egg whites will furnish two dozen of these delicate little cakes, we feel no compunctions, in this day and age, in decreasing the number of eggs called for by simply quartering the recipe.

3 egg whites
½ cup sifted sugar
⅛ teaspoon lemon extract

Beat the egg whites until stiff, add the sifted sugar gradually, beating all the time. Then add the lemon extract — almond extract may be substituted to make a variation — and drop from a teaspoon onto parchment paper which has been wet and then stretched on a board. Waxed paper may be used on a cookie sheet if the other is not available. Bake in a slow oven (300 degrees F.) for about forty-five minutes. By dropping the mixture from a tablespoon and increasing the time of baking somewhat meringues may be made to be used for meringue glacée.

— *Mrs. Tidyman*
(*a guest at Bossis Plantation*)

Nut Cookies

Sugar cookie dough
½ pound walnut or pecan meats
1 teaspoon cinnamon

Make a sugar cookie dough by any favorite recipe and spread it about one-eighth of an inch thick in a large pan. Sprinkle the chopped nuts over the dough very thickly, pressing them down slightly. Then sprinkle the batter with the cinnamon and bake in a moderately hot oven (375 degrees F.) for about fifteen minutes. Cut in squares while still warm.

These cookies have the advantage of not requiring rolling out, and the topping of nuts tastes deliciously toasted. Makes twenty-four two-inch squares.

— *William's Recipe*

GINGER CAKES

- ¼ cup butter
- ½ cup sugar
- ½ cup molasses
- ½ cup milk
- 2 cups flour
- 2 teaspoons ginger

Cream the butter and sugar together. Add the molasses and beat well. Mix and sift the flour and ginger. Add alternately with the milk to the first mixture. Turn into a well-greased shallow pan and bake in a quick oven (425 degrees F.) for about thirty minutes. Cut into squares and serve hot.

The lack of eggs and baking powder makes this cake heavy. While hot, the squares — the amount makes sixteen — are rather good, however, with a pronounced gingery flavor.

— *Miss Harleston's Notebook*

MARVELS

Ten eggs are called for in the original recipe, a difficult number to reduce to present day needs. The recipe also says to add flour enough to make a dough which can be rolled. We found that when this was done the marvels were a little heavy and too solid to be really delectable. They are better when dropped from a teaspoon into the hot fat, drained on brown paper, rolled in powdered sugar and eaten at once.

6 tablespoons sugar
2 eggs, well beaten
$\frac{1}{4}$ teaspoon nutmeg, mace or cinnamon
10 tablespoons flour

Add the sugar to the eggs and beat well. Sift the nutmeg or other spice with the flour and fold into the first mixture. A little more flour may be added if required but we found that this was about the right amount to use for a batter which could be dropped into the hot fat.

Have ready a kettle of fat and drop the batter in by teaspoonfuls. When one side of the little cake is brown, turn it over to brown on the other side. Drain, roll in powdered sugar and serve. This will make about two dozen small cakes.

—*Mary Leize Simons*

French Candy

1 pound powdered sugar
2 egg whites, unbeaten
1 teaspoon vanilla
Figs, nuts and dates

Mix the sugar with the egg whites and flavor with vanilla. Roll out on a sugared board as you would any dough and cut into pieces to cover nuts or dates. Figs should be cut in small pieces before covering.

This uncooked candy may also be used for centers for stuffing dates and prunes and is very good for this purpose. These candies will keep for several days if placed in an airtight tin box.

Makes about three dozen candies.

—*Bossis*

Cocoanut Fudge

3 cups granulated sugar
1 cup milk
3 tablespoons butter
1 cup grated cocoanut
1 teaspoon lemon extract

Put the first four ingredients into a saucepan and stir until the sugar is dissolved. Cook until a soft ball is formed when a little of the mixture is tested in cold water or until 236 degrees F. is reached. Add the lemon extract, but do not stir. When the mixture is lukewarm (110 degrees) beat until thick and creamy. Turn into a buttered pan and mark into diamonds.

—*Mary Leize Simons*

Cocoanut Cakes

3 cups grated cocoanut
1½ cups sugar
2 egg whites

Mix the cocoanut and sugar together and bind with the egg whites. Make into balls with your hands or drop from a teaspoon onto well-greased cookie sheets. Bake in a moderate oven (325 degrees F.) about fifteen minutes. These little cakes are sure to be liked even by those who say that they do not eat cocoanut. Makes two and a half dozen cakes.

—*Mary Leize Simons*

Ground Nut Cake

In spite of its name, this is a candy.

1 quart molasses
1 cup brown sugar
½ cup butter
4 cups peanuts, parched and shelled

Combine the first three ingredients and boil for half an hour over a slow fire. Then add the roasted and shelled peanuts and continue cooking for fifteen minutes. Pour into a lightly greased shallow pan and allow to harden. Break into pieces. This makes a somewhat chewy candy similar to taffy.

Benné cakes are made by substituting benné seed (which is better known in Charleston than in the North) for the peanuts.

— *Carolina Housewife*

Peach Leather I

It is amusing that anything so delicious should bear so dull a name. Peach Leather is the most famous confection of old plantation days. It is dependent on the sun for making, and if possible one should select a week when there is likely to be hot sunshine to make it. If the sun is contrary and refuses to shine, more time must be allowed for exposure of the peach juice to its rays.

4 cups peach puree
1 cup sugar
Powdered sugar

Select very ripe, free-stone peaches, peel them and mash thoroughly. ("Pound in a mortar," the directions read, but few of us have mortars these days!) Put as much of the peach pulp through a sieve as possible and to four cups of this juice and pulp add the granulated sugar. Bring to the boiling point and boil for two minutes. Spread on a dish very thinly and place in the sun for three days as you would in making sunshine strawberry preserves.

When the mixture is thick and leathery — three days will be long enough if the sun is hot — sprinkle with powdered sugar, cut in strips and roll as you would jelly cake. Set the little rolls in the sun for two more days. This should be sufficient to finish drying them. Set on waxed paper and pack in layers in an airtight tin box.

— Miss Rutledge

Peach Leather II

4 quarts peach pulp
4 cups brown sugar
Granulated or powdered sugar

Take a peck or two of soft free-stone peaches, peel and mash them. Press the pulp through a coarse sieve and to four quarts of pulp add one quart of good brown sugar. Mix well together and boil for about two minutes.

Spread the paste on plates and put them in the sun every day until the cakes look dry and will leave the plates readily when a knife is passed around the edges of the cakes. Sprinkle some white sugar over the rough side and roll them up like sweet wafers. If the weather is fine, three days will be enough to dry them.

Apple leather is made in the same manner.

— Carolina Housewife

Butterscotch

1 cup molasses
1 cup sugar
½ cup butter

The sole original directions are "Boil until done"! Put all the ingredients in a saucepan and cook until the crack stage, or 270 degrees, is reached. Turn at once into a lightly buttered pan and mark into squares while still warm. When the candy is cold it can be broken into pieces. This amount makes three dozen squares of a butterscotch with a decided molasses flavor, rather darker than the usual butterscotch but excellent in taste.

—*Mary Leize Simons*

Chocolate Fudge

4 cups sugar
1½ cups milk
2 squares chocolate
¼ cup butter
1 teaspoon vanilla

Put the sugar, milk and grated chocolate into a saucepan and cook, stirring constantly until the sugar is dissolved and the chocolate melted. Then stir occasionally to keep from burning until a little of the mixture dropped in cold water will form a soft ball, or a candy thermometer registers 236 degrees F.).

Remove the pan from the fire and add the butter and vanilla but do not stir. When the candy is lukewarm (110 degrees F.) beat it until thick and creamy. Turn into a buttered pan and mark into squares.

— *Bossis*

Peanut Candy

2 cups shelled peanuts
2 cups granulated sugar

Chop the peanuts fine. Put the sugar into a skillet and stir constantly until it is all melted. Then add the peanuts and pour at once into a buttered pan. When cold, break into pieces.

The finely chopped peanuts make, of course, a much more uniformly nutty candy than the usual peanut brittle. The recipe makes about one pound of candy.

— *Mary Leize Simons*

Benné Brittle

Benné seed cannot be procured in many places, but the candy made with it is so delicious and so characteristic of Charleston that the recipe is here included.

2 cups sugar
½ teaspoon vanilla extract

½ teaspoon lemon extract
2 cups parched benné seed

Add the extracts to the sugar. Melt the sugar in a saucepan, stirring constantly, as for peanut brittle. When the sugar is melted, add the benné seed, stirring it in quickly. Pour at once onto a marble slab to cool or pour into lightly buttered pans. Mark in one-inch squares while still warm and break along the lines when cold.

—*Mrs. Rhett*

Caramels

2 cups sugar
4 squares chocolate, grated
½ cup milk
2 tablespoons butter
1 teaspoon vanilla

Put all the ingredients into a saucepan, stirring until the sugar is dissolved and the chocolate melted. Then let boil without stirring until the firm-ball stage (246 degrees F.) is reached. Remove from the fire and turn at once into a lightly buttered square pan. Do not scrape the saucepan, as the last of the caramel mixture will probably sugar and if this is added to the rest the whole may become granular.

Twenty-four very chocolatey caramels are produced with this recipe.

— *Anna Gray Cart*

Coloring for Icing

Before the days of food colors such as are now sold in the stores, pink icing on a cake was a real achievement. The directions for making red coloring give us some idea of the difficulties encountered:

" To make a red colouring for icing, take twenty grains of cochineal powder, twenty grains of cream of tartar and twenty grains of powdered alum. Put them in a gill of cold soft water and boil it very slowly until reduced to one-half. Strain it through thin muslin and cork it up for use. A very small quantity of this mixture will colour icing a beautiful pink. With pink icing white nonparells should be used."

— ***Miss Leslie***

DESSERTS

AUTOMATIC refrigerators have put their brash, clean faces into Charleston kitchens, but the traditional cooking of the foremothers holds its own. In the high-ceilinged dining-room of Mrs. Goodwyn Rhett's house President Taft ate the same kind of good things that President George Washington ate in his day. And until now the secret recipes of these things have been held closely because they are clannish about their ways in the old city.

If, for example, you should go down there and try to buy a bit of the lacelike old iron work which Italian craftsmen designed for the planters in the days of their wealth, you would be asked, "Are you going to use it in Charleston?" If you say "No," you cannot buy. And until now they have been as chary of giving away their traditional recipes.

The town is full of survivals of the past. But with the coming of concrete roads and tourists, there is a fear that that past may disappear. With real sorrow Charleston saw the passing of the "honey man," who used to sing his wares in these streets of sharp light and shade. He evidently varied his song from day to day. The first version of it I heard was told me by Miss Dorothy Wulbern. It went like this:

Honey, Honey, Honey,
I'se got honey,
You got honey? Yes, ma'am, I'se got honey.
How's you got honey?
I'se got 'em in de comb.
Honey! Honey! Honey!

Essie Woodward Messervey heard him sing another version of his song, this:

Is yo' got honey? Yes, ma'am, I'se got honey.
Is yo' got 'em in de comb? Yes, ma'am, I'se got 'em in de comb.
Is yo' got strained honey? Yes, ma'am, I'se got strained honey.
Is yo' got de debbil shoe string? Yes, ma'am, I'se got de debbil shoe string.
Is yo' got de life evahlastin'? Yes, ma'am, I'se got de life evahlastin'. Honey, Honey, Honey. Is yo' want any honey today?

The old man was all white except for his skin; he wore a white jacket, a white cap on his snowy head, and a white beard. His name was Ralph Bennett, and before he died he was ninety years old and clairvoyant. He told Mrs. Messervey that he could see spirits. Now it happens that none of these recipes in this chapter calls for the use of honey, but what of that? The honey man belongs in Charleston, none the less.

So having paid our respects to the honey man, we pass on to those steamed puddings and whipped cream desserts which are far more important in Charleston than ice creams and ices.

Plum Pudding I

1 pound beef suet
1 pound sugar
8 eggs
1 pound grated stale bread crumbs or half a pound of bread crumbs and half a pound of flour
1 cup brandy or sherry flavoring
2 cups milk
1 pound raisins
1 pound currants
1 nutmeg, grated
2 teaspoons cinnamon
1 teaspoon mace
½ teaspoon salt
Grated rind of 1 large lemon or 1 orange

Chop the suet fine and mix well with the sugar. Add the beaten eggs. If flour is used, dredge the fruit with part of it and mix the spices with the remainder. Add the flour and bread crumbs to the first mixture and then add the liquids and the grated orange or lemon rind. Stir in the fruit and turn into a large, well-greased mold. Steam about three hours.

This makes a very large pudding, which will serve twenty generously. Serve with hard sauce.

For the average family half of this pudding is sufficient. Take half of everything called for and steam for from two to two and a half hours.

Mary Leize Simons

Plum Pudding II

Wine and rye whiskey are called for in the original recipe but we were forced to content ourselves with cooking sherry. In spite of this handicap, this made an excellent pudding. We are giving half of the recipe and this amount will give nearly twenty servings!

½ pound butter
½ pound sugar
3 eggs
2 cups flour
1 teaspoon nutmeg

1 teaspoon cinnamon
½ teaspoon cloves
½ teaspoon mace
1½ pounds currants
1½ pounds raisins
½ pound citron, cut in bits
½ loaf bread
1 pint milk
½ cup sherry flavoring

Cream together the butter and sugar, add the beaten eggs and beat well. Sift the spices with the flour and mix with the fruit. Add to the first mixture. Reduce the bread to crumbs and soak in the milk. Add to the fruit mixture and stir in the sherry. Turn into a well-buttered pudding mold and steam for about two and a half hours. Serve with hard sauce. The pudding may be kept for some time and reheated by steaming just before serving.

—*Dr. Benjamin Huger, Richmond Plantation, Cooper River*

Hard Sauce

If your family is at all fond of hard sauce, double this recipe!

2 tablespoons butter
½ cup confectioners' sugar
1 tablespoon lemon juice

Cream the butter and sugar together well. Add the lemon juice gradually and beat until light.

— *Mary Leize Simons*

Huckleberry Pudding

By using well-drained canned huckleberries in place of the fresh ones, this pudding may be made the year around.

- $\frac{1}{4}$ cup butter
- 1 cup sugar
- 2 eggs
- $1\frac{1}{2}$ cups flour
- 4 teaspoons baking powder
- 1 cup milk
- 2 cups huckleberries

Cream the butter and sugar and add the beaten eggs. Dredge the berries with part of the flour. Sift together the flour and baking powder and add to the first mixture alternately with the milk. Stir the berries into the dough and pour into a well-buttered baking dish. Bake in a moderate oven (350 degrees F.) for about forty-five minutes. Serve with hard sauce.

Sweet Marie Pudding

Although this pudding appears to have no sweetening, the raisins and currants take the place of the missing sugar. The pudding should be served hot with plenty of hard sauce.

2 cups flour
6 teaspoons baking powder
$\frac{1}{4}$ teaspoon salt
1 cup milk
2 eggs
1 tablespoon butter, melted
$\frac{1}{2}$ pound raisins
$\frac{1}{2}$ pound currants

Dredge the raisins and currants with part of the flour and sift the rest with the salt and baking powder. Beat the eggs, add the milk, and combine with the flour. Add the melted butter and last of all the floured fruit. Turn into a well-greased pudding mold and steam for about two hours.

— *Miss C. Blanche Moodie*

Ratifia Cream

Although the basis of this dessert, as of so many Charleston ones, is heavy cream the result is unusual. It is a very rich custard with a distinct flavor of bitter almonds. Not too rich wafers should be served with it. You must accent ratifia on the third syllable (ratifi′a), and eat a very small portion.

3 egg yolks
2 tablespoons cream
2 tablespoons powdered sugar
2 cups heavy cream
3 bitter almonds

Beat the egg yolks, add the two tablespoons of cream and the sugar. Put the two cups of cream and the almonds in a double boiler and bring slowly to the boiling point. Then remove the almonds and add the egg mixture. Stir constantly, always stirring the same way, until the mixture has become quite thick. Remove from the fire and turn into sherbet glasses. This serves six. Laurel leaves may be used in place of the bitter almonds if desired.

Boiled Batter Pudding

This pudding should be eaten while hot. Hard sauce, particularly chocolate hard sauce, is a good accompaniment.

2 tablespoons sugar
3 egg yolks
2 egg whites
¼ cup flour
1 cup milk
¼ teaspoon salt
¼ teaspoon vanilla

Beat the egg yolks well and add the sugar. Then add the flour and salt and when mixed, the milk.

Flavor with the vanilla and, last of all, fold in the stiffly beaten egg whites. Turn into a well-buttered pudding mold and steam for one hour. This will serve six.

—*Miss Harleston's Notebook*

Syllabub I

The recipe given below would serve twelve, and from the time that would be consumed in the making it seems better adapted to the Old South than to this all too hustling time.

To one quart of cream, add half a pint of sweet wine and half a pint of Madeira, the juice of two lemons, a little finely powdered spice and sugar to taste. The peel of the lemons must be steeped in the wine until the flavor is extracted. Whisk all these ingredients together and as the froth rises, take it off with a spoon, lay it upon a fine sieve; what drains from it put into your pan again and whisk it. Put the froth into glasses.

—*Carolina Housewife*

Syllabub II

This is an easily made desert, but the instructions to " take a quart of cream, whites of four eggs, one glass white wine, two small cups powdered sugar " would frighten anyone. However, one-fourth this amount will serve six persons, so it is not such a very extravagant dessert as it at first appears.

1 cup heavy cream
1 egg white
½ cup powdered sugar
2 tablespoons wine flavoring
2 bananas
2 oranges
Powdered sugar

Add half the sugar to the cream and whip until it is stiff. Beat the egg white stiffly and then beat in the remaining sugar. Combine and mix well. Add the wine and pour over the sliced bananas and oranges which have been sweetened to taste. The amount and kind of fruit may be varied to suit the individual taste.

— *Southern Cook Book*

Whips without Eggs

1 cup cream
¾ teaspoon vanilla or ½ teaspoon lemon extract
¼ cup wine flavoring
½ cup powdered sugar

Whip the cream stiffly, flavor with vanilla or lemon. Gradually add the wine flavoring — sherry is customary, but port may be used — and the powdered sugar. Whip again until fairly stiff and serve in tall sherbet glasses with sponge or sour cream cake.

This is a simple dessert and it may be used not only in this way, but also in combination with other desserts to take the place of plain whipped cream.

— *Mary Leize Simons*

Whipped Cream I

1 egg white
$\frac{1}{2}$ cup cream
2 tablespoons sweet port wine flavoring
2 tablespoons sugar

Beat the egg white stiffly and add the cream, wine and sugar. Beat again until stiff and serve in sherbet glasses decorated with a candied cherry, cut in slices. This makes four servings and is one-eighth of the original recipe.

— *Mary Leize Simons*

Whipped Cream II

Not much different from the preceding recipe is this, one of the innumerable whipped cream desserts of Charleston:

1 egg white
1½ tablespoons sugar
1 cup cream
¼ cup sweet cooking sherry or Madeira wine

Combine all the ingredients and whip until stiff. The directions say to take off the froth as it rises and "put on a sieve to drain." This is not necessary if whipping cream is used.

This dessert may be made ahead of time and, in fact, is rather improved by standing, since the wine flavor becomes mellower and more evenly distributed. Served with sponge cake or lady fingers, this makes six servings.

The cream may also be used in place of ordinary whipped cream in almost any recipe.

—*Mary Leize Simons*

Swan's Down Cream

In this near relation to a charlotte russe, the cake is served separately.

⅔ cup heavy cream
1 egg white
⅓ cup sugar
½ teaspoon vanilla

Whip the cream until stiff. Beat the egg white stiffly, add the sugar and combine with the cream.

Flavor with vanilla or with any preferred extract. Beat the mixture for a few minutes and turn into a serving dish. Surround with cracked ice (chilling in the refrigerator for an hour does quite as well) and serve with sponge cake. This will serve four.

—*Mary Leize Simons*

Trifle I

The original recipe calls for three ounces of sugar, but since we used sweetened wine, we found that the sugar could be omitted. It may be added according to taste if this dessert does not seem sweet enough.

1 small sponge cake, sliced
1 cup heavy cream
½ cup milk
¾ cup wine flavoring

Put the sliced sponge cake into a dish and moisten with wine flavoring—about one-fourth cup should be sufficient. Combine the milk and three-fourths cup of wine with one-half cup of cream and mix well. Pour about half of this mixture over the cake. Then whip the rest, adding the remaining cream, until it is stiff and place on top of the cake. Serves six to eight. This is attractive when put into sherbet glasses and served with lady fingers.

—*Miss Harleston's Notebook*

Trifle II

This is a rather elaborate dessert with a pronounced wine flavor. Lay in the bottom of a glass dessert bowl a quarter of a pound of macaroons and a few slices of sponge cake. Wet them thoroughly with sweet wine flavoring. Whip together the following ingredients: One pint of cream, one-half cup of milk, one cup of Teneriffe wine (port wine flavoring will do as a substitute), the grated rind of one lemon and the juice of half a lemon, and one-eighth teaspoon each of cinnamon, nutmeg and mace, adding sugar to taste. As the froth arises, take it off and lay it upon the cake until the dish is full.

"A custard may be put first upon the cake," the recipe suggests, "and the froth laid lightly upon that." This makes an even richer dessert but the flavor is delightful.

Snow Cream

This popular whipped cream dessert of Charleston serves from ten to fifteen.

Sponge cake
Wine flavoring
3 egg whites
2 tablespoons powdered sugar
½ cup sweet wine
1 pint heavy cream

Put thin slices of sponge cake in the bottom of a dish and moisten with wine. Beat the egg whites stiffly and add the remaining ingredients. Beat these well and pour over cake. Allow to stand for a short time in the refrigerator before serving.

Lemon Pudding

The recipe has been in Miss Georgia Porter's family for seventy-five years.

1 dozen lady fingers
2 lemons
1 cup granulated sugar
2 tablespoons butter
3 egg yolks
2 egg whites
1½ cups powdered sugar

Crumble the sponge cake and grate the rinds of two lemons into it and add the juice of one and one-half lemons. Mix the butter, sugar and egg yolks (do not beat them), adding them to the crumbled cake. Bake in a moderate oven (350 degrees F.) until light brown and set aside to cool.

Beat the whites of two eggs and flavor with the juice of half a lemon, adding gradually one and one-half cups of powdered sugar. Ice over the pudding and bake in a slow oven (300 degrees F.)

to a buff color. This will take about twelve minutes.

This amount of sugar makes a very sugary and sweet meringue. The pudding will serve six and is delicious in flavor.

— *Georgia L. Porter*

Charlotte Russe I

1 cup heavy cream
1 cup powdered sugar
1 tablespoon gelatin
1 cup milk
6 almond macaroons
½ teaspoon vanilla
¼ teaspoon almond extract
Sponge cake

Add the cream gradually to the sugar, rubbing them together until perfectly smooth. Soak the gelatin in three tablespoons of cold milk and dissolve in the remaining milk which has been scalded. Let cool and add to the first mixture to which have been added the crumbs from the crushed macaroons (the macaroons must be stale to crush easily). Flavor with the vanilla and almond extract and beat until quite thick. Line a mold with sponge cake, cut thin, and after the mixture becomes stiffened, turn it in.

While this is the traditional method, the time of

beating may be reduced by whipping the cream before adding the other ingredients. More beating will be necessary at the end but much less than if all the whipping is done by hand. Serves eight, generously.

— *William's Recipe*

Charlotte Russe II

1 cup heavy cream
1 cup powdered sugar
1 tablespoon gelatin
1 cup milk
2 egg whites
1 teaspoon vanilla
Sponge cake

This charlotte russe is made in the same manner as William's. Add the cream gradually to the sugar, rubbing them together until perfectly smooth. Soak the gelatin in three tablespoons of cold milk and dissolve in the remaining milk which has been scalded. Let cool and add to the first mixture. Beat the egg whites stiffly and fold in. Flavor with the vanilla and beat for a long time, until the mixture is stiff. Turn into a mold lined with thin slices of sponge cake and let chill thoroughly. Serves eight.

The original recipe reads:

" One pint very thick cream, rub up smooth with

one pint of powdered sugar. Dissolve a half of box of gelatin into a pint of fresh milk and when cold rub it into the cream. Then add the whites of four eggs beaten to a stiff froth. Flavor with vanilla and beat for a long time. Line a mould with sponge cake. The mixture must be solid before it is put into the mould."

—*Miss Mitchell*

Charlotte Russe III

This is more like the charlotte russe found in the North.

1 cup milk
2 eggs
½ cup sugar
2 cups cream
2 tablespoons gelatin
1½ teaspoons vanilla
Lady fingers

Make a custard of the sugar, eggs and milk, saving out one-fourth cup of milk in which to soak the gelatin. Dissolve the soaked gelatin in the hot custard. Beat the cream until stiff, fold in the custard-gelatin mixture and flavor with the vanilla. Line a mold with lady fingers, split in two, and when the charlotte thickens put it in the mold and cover with more lady fingers. Chill thoroughly.

When stiff, loosen the sides of the mold with a knife and turn it out. Serves ten.

—*Miss Rutledge's Cook Book*

Charlotte Russe IV

½ tablespoon gelatin
½ cup cold milk
3 eggs, separated
1¼ cups powdered sugar
2 cups cream, whipped
1 teaspoon vanilla
Sponge cake

Soak the gelatin in the cold milk. Beat the yolks of three eggs and the powdered sugar together. Dissolve the gelatin, placing the metal cup in which it is soaked in a pan of hot water and stirring until all the little particles are dissolved. Whip the cream and add the dissolved gelatin. Then add the beaten egg yolks and sugar and then the stiffly beaten egg whites. Flavor with the vanilla or substitute rose extract if preferred. Line a deep pudding dish with sliced sponge cake, pour in the mixture and set aside until firm. Serves ten to twelve.

—*Mary Leize Simons*

Orange Jelly

"Take the juice of eight oranges and six lemons; grate the peel of half the fruit and steep it in a pint of cold water. When the flavor is extracted mix the water with the juice. Add one cup of melted sugar, one package gelatin melted, and the beaten whites of seven eggs. Put all in a saucepan and stir until it boils. Let it boil a few minutes. Put it in a mold or in glasses. Set in refrigerator and serve when set."

Although this is called "orange jelly" it is as much lemon in flavor. We did not find the amount of sugar given enough unless the dessert was served with very sweet whipped cream, in which case the tartness of the jelly combined perfectly with the sweet, bland cream.

For eight servings we found the following quantities sufficient:

1 cup orange juice
½ cup lemon juice
Grated rind of 2 oranges
Grated rind of 1½ lemons
1 cup water
¾ cup sugar
1⅓ tablespoons gelatin
3 egg whites

Simmer the grated orange and lemon rinds for about ten minutes. Soak the gelatin in three tablespoons of orange juice and dissolve in the hot water in which the grated rinds have been simmered. Add the sugar and stir until dissolved. The grated rinds may be strained out — partially, at least — if preferred, or left in for a more pronounced flavor. Add the gelatin mixture to the fruit juices. Beat the egg whites stiffly and fold in the fruit juices. Pour into a mold or into glasses. Set in the refrigerator and chill thoroughly.

— *Miss Rutledge's Cook Book*

Strawberry Nonsense

2 cups milk
½ cup sugar
½ teaspoon vanilla
1 tablespoon gelatin
Sponge cake
Sugar
1 quart strawberries
3 egg whites
½ cup powdered sugar

Soak the gelatin in two tablespoons of the milk. Bring the rest of the milk to the boiling point, add the sugar and vanilla, and dissolve the gelatin in the hot milk. Line a deep dish with thin slices of stale sponge cake, pour in part of the gelatin mixture, put in a thick layer of hulled strawberries, sprinkle with sugar, then add more cake, berries and sugar. Let the top layer be of cake and pour the gelatin mixture over all. Set in the refrigerator to become firm. The amount of sugar to be sprinkled over the berries depends upon their sweetness.

When the pudding is firm, turn it out and garnish with a meringue made of the egg whites and powdered sugar, decorating it with choice berries. Whipped cream might be used in place of the meringue. This will serve six generously.

—*Southern Cook Book*

Chocolate Sponge

Fantastic and ebullient are the colors that flare out of the moss-hung oaks of Middleton Place Gardens, to which so many thousands of people come each brilliant spring. The recipe below was given to us by the owner of these Gardens, who has the ineffable delight of being able to look across their glowing acres whenever he wishes, these acres which are as famous in Europe as they are in America.

1½ tablespoons gelatin
⅓ cup cold water
½ cup boiling water
4 eggs, separated
1 cup granulated sugar
4 squares melted chocolate
1 teaspoon vanilla
Whipped cream

Soak the gelatin in the cold water for ten minutes; then dissolve it in the boiling water. Beat the egg yolks and the sugar until they are very creamy and add the melted chocolate, beating it in thoroughly. Add one teaspoon of vanilla and beat again. Then stir in the gelatin.

Beat the egg whites very stiffly and fold in the chocolate mixture. Turn into a large dish or into individual dishes and chill in the refrigerator. It will be ready to serve in about an hour. Cover with sweetened whipped cream, before serving. This delicious dessert will serve six. It is really quite rich but it " slips down " with remarkable ease!

—*Henningham Ellet Smith, Middleton Place, Ashley River Road*

Coffee Soufflé

1½ cups coffee
½ cup milk
⅔ cup sugar
¼ teaspoon salt
3 eggs, separated
1 tablespoon gelatin
½ teaspoon vanilla

Soften the gelatin in two tablespoons of cold milk. Mix the coffee, the remainder of the milk and half of the sugar and heat in a double boiler. Add the remaining sugar and salt to the yolks of the eggs, slightly beaten. Add carefully to the scalding liquid and cook, stirring constantly, until the mixture thickens. As soon as the custard coats the spoon remove it from the fire, for it thickens only slightly. Add the softened gelatin and stir until dissolved. When cold, and beginning to stiffen, add the whites of the eggs, beaten until stiff. Add the vanilla, turn into a mold or put in individual sherbet glasses, chill thoroughly and serve with whipped cream. Serves six generously.

— *Anita De Saussure*

Wine Jelly

Although this recipe cannot be tried, yet it is a famous one, for Mrs. Martha Laurens Patterson's mother used to make quantities of it to give to friends who were sick. Possibly by decreasing the sugar one could make it by using one of the sweet cooking wines.

2 packages gelatin
1 quart cold water
1 quart boiling water
1 quart wine
4 lemons, sliced
4 egg whites, stiffly beaten, also shells
1 teaspoon ground mace
1 teaspoon ground nutmeg

1 teaspoon ground cloves
1 teaspoon ground allspice
2 sticks cinnamon
1 quart sugar

Boil ten minutes. Strain through flannel.

—*Martha Laurens Patterson*

Rice Pudding

2 cups milk
2-inch stick of cinnamon
$\frac{1}{4}$ cup butter
$\frac{1}{3}$ cup sugar
4 eggs
$\frac{1}{2}$ cup soft boiled rice
$\frac{3}{4}$ cup raisins

Scald the milk with the cinnamon. Remove the cinnamon and add the butter and sugar. Add the milk slowly to the slightly beaten eggs and stir in the other ingredients. The raisins may be omitted if preferred, but most persons think they improve the pudding. Turn the mixture into a buttered pudding dish and bake in a slow oven (300 degrees F.) until the custard is firm and top browned, about forty-five minutes. The pudding will serve six and is (a seeming paradox) both delicate and substantial.

—*Mary Leize Simons*

Lemon Meringue

In reading this recipe, one might think it a bread pudding, but in tasting it such a suspicion would never occur!

- 2 cups bread crumbs
- Juice and grated rind of 1½ lemons
- ½ cup water
- 2 eggs, separated
- ¾ cup sugar
- ⅓ cup butter

The bread should be fresh and only the inside of the loaf used. Break the bread into small pieces and measure two cups. Pour the cold water over the grated lemon rind and let stand while the butter and sugar are creamed together and the egg yolks beaten in. Mix the lemon juice with the grated rind and water and either add to the bread crumbs or add alternately with the crumbs to the butter mixture. In either case, the liquid must be added carefully to avoid a separation of the butter into little particles. This does not by any means spoil the pudding, however, even if it does occur. Turn into a buttered pudding dish and bake in a moderate oven (350 degrees F.) for about twenty-five minutes. Remove from the oven, cover with a meringue made of the egg whites, beaten stiff with four tablespoons of sugar, and return to a slow oven (300 degrees F.) for twelve minutes to brown the meringue. Serve cold. This is a very rich pudding, although the amount of butter given in this recipe is less than is called for in the original recipe.

Pineapple Pudding

$\frac{1}{3}$ cup butter
$\frac{1}{2}$ cup sugar
2 eggs, separated
1 cup bread crumbs
1 cup grated pineapple

Cream the butter and sugar, add the beaten egg yolks, then the bread crumbs and fruit, and lastly fold in the stiffly beaten egg whites. Turn into a buttered pudding dish and bake in a moderate oven (325 degrees F.) for about thirty-five minutes. Canned pineapple may be used for this dessert in place of the fresh fruit, but then the sugar should be decreased. Six small servings.

Wine Sauce for Sponge Cake

$\frac{1}{2}$ cup butter
1 cup sugar
1 cup sweet port flavoring
$\frac{1}{2}$ cup boiling water
$\frac{1}{4}$ teaspoon nutmeg

Cream the butter and sugar together well and add the other ingredients. Stir well together and serve over cake. The original recipe calls for two cups of sugar, but in these Prohibition days of sweetened wines, this made far too sweet a sauce.

—*Mary Leize Simons*

Queen of Puddings

3 tablespoons butter
1½ cups granulated sugar
5 eggs, separated
2 cups fine, dry bread crumbs
1 quart milk
1 teaspoon vanilla
½ cup jelly
½ cup sugar

Cream the butter and sugar together and add the well-beaten yolks of the eggs. Beat well and add the bread crumbs which have been soaked in the milk, and then the vanilla. Stir well and turn into a large pudding dish, well buttered. The dish should be about two-thirds full. Bake in a moderate oven (350 degrees F.) until the custard is set, from thirty-five to forty minutes. Then spread the top of the pudding with jelly, jam or any preserved fruit and cover with a meringue made of the egg whites and the one-half cup of sugar. Bake in a slow oven (300 degrees F.) until the meringue is brown, about twelve minutes. Serve cold with cream or custard sauce.

This pudding is worthy of its name. It will serve about ten and may be varied by using fresh fruit for the preserves.

—*Mrs. Bennett*

Cottage Pudding

½ cup sugar
1½ tablespoons butter
2 eggs
½ cup sweet milk
1½ cups flour
2 teaspoons baking powder
¼ teaspoon salt

Cream the butter and sugar together and add the well-beaten eggs. Mix and sift the dry ingredients and add alternately with the milk to the first mixture. Turn into a well-greased cake pan and bake in a moderate oven (350 degrees F.) for about thirty-five minutes. Serve hot with a sauce. This serves six generously.

—*Bossis*

Sauce for Cottage Pudding

1 cup sugar
1 tablespoon flour
½ tablespoon butter
2 egg yolks
1 cup boiling water
2 tablespoons wine flavoring
¼ teaspoon nutmeg

Mix the sugar and flour well, cream in the butter and add the eggs, beating well. Then add the boiling water gradually, stirring all the time, and cook until the mixture thickens. Remove from the fire and add the wine and nutmeg. Serve hot with cottage pudding.

—*Mary Leize Simons*

Fudge Sauce

2 cups white sugar
1 cup brown sugar
1 cup cocoa
3 tablespoons flour
¼ cup butter
1½ cups water
½ teaspoon vanilla

Mix the dry ingredients thoroughly and add the butter and water. Bring to the boiling point and cook until thick — about ten minutes. Add the vanilla. This is good served hot or cold over ice cream or cake. Makes about one pint of sauce.

— Anita De Saussure

Tapioca Cream

$\frac{1}{3}$ cup instant tapioca
1 quart milk
3 egg yolks
$\frac{1}{2}$ cup sugar
1 teaspoon lemon or vanilla extract
3 egg whites
6 tablespoons sugar

Scald the milk, add the tapioca and cook in the top of a double boiler for fifteen minutes, stirring frequently. Beat the egg yolks well, add the sugar and beat again. Combine gradually with the milk and tapioca mixture and return to the fire until the eggs are cooked and the mixture slightly thickened — about two minutes. Flavor and turn into a pudding dish and cover with a meringue made of the egg whites and sugar. Bake in a slow oven (300 degrees F.) for twelve minutes to brown the meringue. This will serve eight. We found that adding one-half teaspoon of salt to the scalded milk improved the flavor of the pudding.

— Mary Leize Simons

Cocoanut Tarts

You can understand why Charleston cooks have been so clever in preparing the shellfish from surrounding waters, why they were so especially clever with the rice which was grown near by and with the wild birds which are profuse in their marshes. But you are surprised at the wonderful things they do with cocoanuts until you remember that centuries ago, when Charleston was a great seaport and cocoanuts were yet rare in most American markets, this nut-flavored food was brought in considerable quantities by traders from the West Indies, and that moreover many of Charleston's early settlers came from the Barbadoes.

½ cup butter
1¼ cups powdered sugar
6 egg yolks
3 egg whites
1 teaspoon nutmeg
2 cups grated cocoanut
Pastry

Cream the butter and sugar together thoroughly and add the egg yolks and whites, which have been beaten together. Then add the nutmeg and the cocoanut. Line small patty pans with rich pastry — puff paste may be used, although it is not necessary — and put in the filling. Bake in a moderate oven (350 degrees F.) for thirty minutes. These little tarts are very rich and "gooey" and most delicious.

—Mrs. Tidyman

Cocoanut Pudding

¼ cup butter
1 cup sugar
1 tablespoon water
1 cup grated cocoanut
1 tablespoon finely cut citron
Grated rind and juice of half a lemon
4 eggs

Mix the butter, sugar and water in a saucepan and boil for two minutes. Let this cook, then add the cocoanut, citron and the grated rind and juice of the half lemon. Add the well-beaten egg yolks and, last of all, fold in the stiffly beaten egg whites. Bake in paper cases or in individual dishes in a moderate oven (350 degrees F.) for about twenty-five minutes. Do not allow the mixture to stand, but bake at once.

—Southern Cook Book

Delmonico Peaches

This peach and apple combination may be served with the meat course or, topped with whipped cream, may be eaten either hot or cold for dessert.

3 medium-sized apples
1 No. 2 can peaches
4 double almond macaroons
2 ounces blanched almonds
1 tablespoon butter

Pare the apples and cut them in quarters. Cook the apples in the juice from the can of peaches until soft. Then add the peaches and continue cooking until both fruits are soft enough to mash. Mash them well with the potato masher.

Chop the almonds very fine and roll or grind the macaroons. Butter a baking dish and put in a layer of peach and apple. Sprinkle with a mixture of almond and macaroon crumbs, dot with bits of butter and put in another layer of peach and apple. Continue until the ingredients are used, having the almond and macaroon mixture on top.

Bake in a moderate oven (350 degrees F.) until the top is brown, about forty minutes. This will make eight servings.

While this is delicious with almost any meat course, it is especially good with turkey, duck or quail.

—*Eunice Hunter Clark*

Apple Charlotte I

This recipe for Apple Charlotte makes my favorite dessert. It was given to me by Miss Leize

Dawson, owner of the Villa Margherita. It is a most elastic recipe, good with or without meringue, and delicious with either peaches or apples.

3 large apples, sliced thin
Granulated sugar
5 slices buttered bread or toast
Juice of one orange
Juice of half a lemon
½ cup orange marmalade
Meringue

Butter a baking dish and put in a layer of thinly sliced apples. Sprinkle with sugar — the amount depends upon the tartness of the apples — and cover with a layer of buttered bread. If the crusts are removed from the bread the pudding is daintier. Add another layer of apples and sugar and sprinkle with the lemon and orange juice mixed. Spread the remaining bread liberally with orange marmalade, reserving a little of the marmalade for the meringue. Bake in a moderate oven for about forty-five minutes.

Make a meringue of two or three egg whites, allowing two tablespoons of sugar to each white, and heap upon the pudding. Dot with orange marmalade and return to the oven, which should now be slow (300 degrees F.) for twelve minutes to brown the meringue. This serves six.

— *Miss Leize Dawson*

Apple Charlotte II

Another recipe for Apple Charlotte somehow slipped over into this book from Georgia, which is so close to Charleston that recipes are constantly interchanged. It was given to us by Julia Collier Harris, the daughter-in-law of Joel Chandler Harris, in whose home all the great people who visited Georgia were entertained. Julia Harris and her husband, Julian, have been awarded the Pulitzer Prize for distinguished service in journalism.

1 pound cooking apples
1 cup sugar
Water
2 tablespoons lime syrup
5 slices buttered bread

Pare and core the apples and cut them into slices. Stew with the sugar and about one cup of water, stirring occasionally. When the apples are tender add the lime syrup. (This may be made by cooking lime juice and sugar together for a few minutes, using three tablespoons of lime juice to one-fourth cup of sugar.)

Butter a baking dish and line it with buttered bread from which the crusts have been removed. Then put in a layer of apples and one of buttered bread, continuing until the ingredients are used. The top layer should be of apples. Bake in a moderate oven (350 degrees F.) for about twenty-five minutes. Serves four. Hard sauce is very good with this pudding.

—*Julia Collier Harris*

Apple Snow

6 apples
3 egg whites
Sugar
½ teaspoon lemon juice
Custard sauce

Pare, core and slice the apples and cook them in as little water as possible until soft. Cool, strain and add to the well-beaten egg whites. Sweeten to taste and whip well until the eggs and apples are thoroughly blended and the pudding holds up in "points." Then flavor — cinnamon or nutmeg may be substituted for the lemon juice, if preferred. Pile in sherbet glasses and serve with a soft custard sauce. This will serve eight generously.

—*Mary Leize Simons*

White Compote of Apples

6 large apples
2 cups water
½ cup sugar
Juice of ½ lemon
Cream cheese

Cut the apples in half, peel them and take out the seeds. Make a syrup of the water, sugar and lemon juice and stew the apples gently in it until they are tender. When the apples are soft but unbroken, remove them from the syrup and arrange in a dessert dish. Let the syrup keep on boiling until it is clear and rich; then pour it over the apples.

Cool and serve with soft cream cheese. This makes an excellent finish for a hearty meal.

— *Madame de Genlis' Recipe*

Strawberry Shortcake

$\frac{1}{4}$ cup shortening
$\frac{3}{4}$ cup sugar
2 eggs
$\frac{1}{2}$ cup milk or water
$1\frac{1}{2}$ cups pastry flour
$2\frac{1}{2}$ teaspoons baking powder
$\frac{1}{4}$ teaspoon salt
1 quart strawberries
$\frac{1}{2}$ pint cream

Cream the shortening, add the sugar gradually. Separate the eggs. Beat the yolks until creamy, add to the butter and sugar mixture and mix well. Sift the flour, measure, add the baking powder and salt and sift again. Add the flour and milk alternately. Beat the whites of the eggs until stiff and fold into the mixture. Pour into two well-greased layer cake pans and bake in a moderate oven (350 degrees F.) for about twenty-five minutes. Remove cake from the pans. Spread one cake with a layer of sweetened crushed strawberries. Cover with the other cake and cover the whole with more fruit. Spread whipped cream over the top. Serves six.

Prune Peachy

If there is any difficulty in persuading the family to eat their allotment of prunes, serve them in this fashion and we predict that they will all disappear!

½ pound uncooked prunes
1½ cups prune juice
½ cup sugar
1 stick cinnamon
½ cup cornstarch
1½ cups cold water
1 tablespoon lemon juice
Cream

Pick over and wash prunes. Soak one hour in cold water and cook the prunes until soft in the same water. There should be one and a half cups of the prune juice left after boiling. Remove the stones from the prunes, add the sugar, cinnamon and prune juice, and boil for ten minutes. Mix the cornstarch with the cold water, add the prunes and boil for five minutes. Remove the cinnamon, add the lemon juice and turn into a mold. Let cool and chill thoroughly in the refrigerator. Serve with cream, either whipped or plain. Sufficient for six servings.

—*Mary Heyward*

Ambrosia

A Charleston variation of the old stand-by of cut-up oranges and cocoanut has a new twist or two.

6 oranges
1 pineapple
1 large cocoanut, grated
Powdered sugar

Select sweet oranges and peel and slice them, freeing them of seeds. Peel the pineapple and shred it. Arrange in a large dessert bowl alternate layers of sliced oranges and shredded pineapple with the grated cocoanut and powdered sugar sprinkled over each layer.

—*Mary Leize Simons*

Blackberry Pudding

If canned berries are used, they should be well drained. We used loganberries and found them very successful.

2 cups blackberries
$1\frac{1}{2}$ cups flour
$\frac{1}{2}$ teaspoon soda
$\frac{1}{4}$ teaspoon salt
$\frac{1}{2}$ cup New Orleans molasses

Mix and sift the dry ingredients, stir in the berries and add the molasses. Mix well, turn into a buttered pudding dish and bake in a moderate oven (375 degrees F.) for about half an hour. This serves six. A hard sauce is suggested to accompany this dessert.

—*Mary Leize Simons*

Fresh Fig Ice Cream

1 pint cream
1 pint milk
6 eggs, separated
1 cup sugar
2 tablespoons sherry
1 quart fresh figs, peeled

Scald the milk and cream together. Beat the yolks of eggs and sugar until very light. Then beat the whites to a stiff froth. Pour the hot milk over the sugar and egg yolks, stirring continuously. Then add the stiffly beaten egg whites, mix thoroughly and add the sherry. Last of all stir in the figs. Cool and freeze.

The amount of sugar required will vary with the sweetness of the figs and will depend upon whether or not sweetened sherry is used. Less sugar will be needed with the sweet sherry than is called for in the recipe.

—*Mrs. L. D. Simonds*

Frozen Custard

1 quart milk
3 eggs
1 cup sugar
2 teaspoons vanilla

Scald the milk, add the slightly beaten eggs which have been mixed with the sugar, being very careful that they do not curdle. Cook until the mixture coats the spoon, stirring constantly. Let cool, add the vanilla and freeze, using three parts of ice to one of salt.

While this custard is not rich enough to take the place of ice cream, it is smooth in texture and is an excellent base for ice cream sauces, far better, in fact, than the richer creams.

—*Mary Leize Simons*

Pineapple Ice

4 cups water
2½ cups sugar

1 cup orange juice
1 cup grated pineapple
(juice and pulp)

Heat two cups of water to boiling and turn over the sugar, stirring until the sugar is dissolved. Add the orange juice and pineapple together with two cups of ice cold water. Cool and freeze, using three parts ice to one of salt.

The ice is cream color, with flecks of yellow pineapple. The pineapple gives the predominant flavor, but the elusive taste of orange makes it out of the ordinary. Makes about two and a half quarts of ice.

—*Mary Leize Simons*

Apple Fritters

3 medium-sized apples
½ cup "good brandy" or cooking sherry
¼ teaspoon cinnamon
1½ cups flour
1 tablespoon baking powder
1 tablespoon sugar
¼ teaspoon salt
1 egg
⅔ cup milk

Select fine, sound apples, peel and core them neatly. Cut each into six equal round slices. Place them in a dish, pour the sherry over them, adding the cinnamon to it, and let them stand for two hours. Each piece of apple should be turned so that it will absorb part of the wine flavoring. Drain them well, being careful to keep each piece whole and save the liquid for further use. Prepare a batter by mixing and sifting the flour with the baking powder, sugar and salt, adding the egg well beaten and combining with the milk. Dip each slice of apple in the batter separately and drop one by one into hot fat, removing them with a skimmer as soon as they are golden brown. Two minutes should be sufficient to cook them properly. Let the fritters drain for a moment on brown paper to remove the superfluous grease. If served with the meat course, omit powdered sugar and sauce. If they are to be served as dessert, however, dredge the fritters with powdered sugar and serve with a sauce made using the sherry drained from the apples.

For the sauce use:

$\frac{3}{4}$ cup water
$\frac{1}{2}$ cup sherry or brandy or both
Sugar to taste
$\frac{1}{2}$ teaspoon grated nutmeg

Mix the ingredients, heat to the boiling point and serve very hot.

—*Mrs. E. H. Sparkman*

Fruit Puffs

First cousins to "apple turnovers" are the southern fruit puffs. Make a rich puff paste and cut it in squares. Place a spoonful of stewed fruit or preserves on each square and fold it over in a triangle, pressing the edges down well. Bake in a quick oven (425 degrees F.) until the pastry is browned.

—*Miss Mitchell*

Cream Puffs

1 cup boiling water
½ cup butter
1 cup sifted flour
3 eggs

Boil the water and butter together and as soon as the butter is melted add the flour all at once. Stir briskly until the mass will leave the sides of the pan. Remove from the fire and beat in the eggs, one at a time, beating thoroughly after each addition. Drop by spoonfuls on a well-buttered baking sheet. The puffs should be far enough apart so that there is no danger of their touching and they should be slightly heaped in the center. Bake in a quick oven (425 degrees F.) until no moisture appears on the outside of the puffs. As long as any drop of moisture shows, there is danger that the puffs will collapse after being taken from the oven. This makes about a dozen puffs.

For the filling, dissolve six tablespoons of cornstarch in one cup of milk. Heat the mixture and add one egg beaten with one-half cup of sugar. Cook until thick, stirring constantly, and add one-half teaspoon vanilla. When the puffs and filling have cooled, open the side of each puff with a sharp knife and fill it. Dust the tops of the cream puffs with confectioners' sugar.

—Mrs. W. E. Turner

Puff Pudding

By no stretch of the imagination could this be termed an economical pudding, not with eggs at their usual altitude. But it is so delicious that one is willing now and then to sacrifice five eggs to the cause.

5 eggs, separated
¾ cup flour
2 cups milk
½ teaspoon salt

Beat the yolks of the eggs well and add gradually the flour which has been mixed to a thin paste with the milk. Stir in the salt and add some flavoring if desired. Turn into a casserole and bake in a moderately hot oven (375 degrees F.) for half an hour. Serve with any preferred sauce. A cherry sauce is very good with this pudding, or the more customary chocolate sauce may be used.

—*Mary Leize Simons*

Transparent Pies

½ cup butter
2 cups sugar
5 eggs
½ teaspoon nutmeg
   or juice of 1 lemon
Pastry

Cream the butter and sugar and add the eggs slightly beaten and the chosen flavoring. Line individual cake pans with pastry and pour in the mixture. Bake in a moderate oven (325 degrees F.) for twenty minutes. This makes fifteen tarts.

Mincemeat

Obvious reasons prevent our testing this recipe in the Prohibition Year of Our Lord 1930, but if the ingredients were available, we feel confident that this would make a mincemeat which one would be glad to risk dreams of many grandmothers to eat!

1 beef tongue, boiled and chopped very fine
2 pounds raisins
2 pounds suet, chopped fine
1 pound citron, chopped fine
1 dozen apples, chopped fine
2 pounds sugar
1 quart wine
1 pint whiskey
Cinnamon, nutmeg and mace to taste

Mix all and set in a stone crock until ready for pies.

— *Nieuport Plantation, Combahee River*

Pumpkin Pie

1 cup stewed pumpkin
1 cup brown sugar
1 teaspoon ground ginger
1 teaspoon ground cinnamon
¼ teaspoon salt
2 eggs
2 cups milk
2 tablespoons melted butter
Pastry

Add the sugar and seasonings to the pumpkin and mix well. Then add the slightly beaten eggs and the milk and last of all stir in the melted butter. Turn into a pie plate lined with pastry and bake in a hot oven (425 degrees F.) for five minutes. Then lower the heat to moderate (350 degrees F.) and bake until the filling is set. A knife inserted into the center of the pie should come out clean when the pie is done. The pie should be thoroughly cold when served.

—*Miss Bennett*

Buttermilk Custard Pie

3 eggs, separated
½ cup sugar (about)
¾ cup butter
3 tablespoons flour
2 cups buttermilk
Grated rind of 1 lemon
Pastry

Cream the butter and sugar and add the well-beaten egg yolks. Add the flour, grated lemon rind and then the buttermilk. Fold in the stiffly beaten egg whites and turn into two pie pans lined with pastry. The crust should be baked in a hot oven for fifteen minutes before putting in the filling.

Bake in a moderately hot oven (375 degrees F.) for about forty minutes. If the milk is very sour, add more sugar. We found that two-thirds of a cup of sugar was needed when we tested this recipe.

—*Mrs. A. H. Lyons*

Blackberry Jelly

This spiced jelly makes an excellent accompaniment for meats and it is an especially happy combination with cream cheese to serve as dessert at the end of a hearty meal.

For each quart of blackberries allow the following spices:

- 3/8 teaspoon cinnamon
- 1/4 teaspoon nutmeg
- 1/4 teaspoon mace
- 1/8 teaspoon cloves

Wash the berries, add the spices and cook them gently until soft, stirring frequently to crush them and to prevent burning. Squeeze through a jelly bag and put the juice again through a bag, using a flannel one the second time. If a clear jelly is desired, the bag must not be squeezed. For each pint of juice add one pound of sugar and let it simmer over a slow fire until a little will jelly when dropped on a cold plate. Turn into jelly glasses, cover with a thin coating of paraffin and allow to cool. When the jelly is cold, pour on another layer of paraffin, turning each glass so that the paraffin will run well up on the sides of the glass, and insure a perfect seal.

—*Miss Mitchell*

BEVERAGES

It is said of Charleston ladies that their names appear in Charleston newspapers only three times in their lives — when they are born, when they are married and when they die. No social function of importance except a wedding or a funeral is ever mentioned in any of its newspapers. You look in vain in their columns for the doings of names of great tradition. The esoteric cooking, the stately dinner, are therefore kept close and quiet. It is for this reason that, though you have heard about the restaurants of New Orleans, you have heard little of the cooking in Charleston, even though there are two or three small tearooms and an inn which cook in the traditional manner.

Naturally, in a place which for centuries has cultivated a taste for fine food, there is equally a taste for fine liquors. Indeed, they are taken for granted, as they are everywhere among epicures. In one of the many volumes of Marcel Proust's rhythmic life-work, there is a long and detailed account of a perfect dinner. Several chapters are required to describe the guests and the details of the food, from the marketing for it to its cooking and its consumption. In all that account no mention is made of wine or liqueurs. It is assumed that the proper drinks were served with each course.

So in Charleston you assume that you will have the special drink which belongs with its food. The land is rich in advice about how to make peach brandy and such, but these we cannot give here. We cannot give them even by the device of that manufacturer who sold grains with a book of instructions which read: "Be careful not to do so and so, because if you do, you will have beer." But I have heard somewhere, it seems to me, that people are able to get the alcoholic ingredients needed for these recipes without making them.

One jessamine-scented night we drove with a group of charming people to the Otranto Club, an old plantation house about ten miles from Charleston, where we sat about a fire and sang songs. And whether it was because we drank the famous punch described below, or for some other reason, before the evening was over the party turned into an unpremeditated and unforgettable concert.

Otranto Club Punch

This punch, as made at Otranto Club, is one of the things we must be content to read about but not expect to taste. It makes such interesting reading, however, that we have included it.

For a party of thirty: Dissolve one pound of sugar (loaf sugar preferred) in one quart of strong green tea, the juice of twelve lemons, strained, one pint of peach brandy, one quart of Jamaica rum, two quarts of California brandy or good rye whiskey. Serve with an abundance of ice, adding a liberal quantity of Apollinaris or White Rock water to suit the taste.

To make Rhine wine punch, leave out the tea and use Rhine wine or sauterne for the base.

A few slices of orange floating in the bowl helps the appearance and flavor, and a slight addition of raspberry syrup for sweetening is preferred by some.

Noyan

Mary A. Sparkman, who contributes this recipe, writes, "Noyan must have been a favorite beverage, judging from the frequency with which the recipes for it appear in the old books. The quaint wording of this one and the writing itself indicate its age, as well as dates in the book, the earliest of which is 1773. The book was handed down to my grandmother, Mrs. P. C. Kirk, Loch Dhu Plantation, Upper St. John's, Berkeley County, S. C."

Take of peach kernels two ounces. Alcohol and water each a half pint. White sugar eight ounces. Blanch your kernels first, then beat with the sugar to a paste. Add the diluted alcohol and suffer it to stand for a week, then filter and you will have a delightful cordial.

Orange Cordial

Another recipe doomed to go untried reads: "Take the thinnest parings of fifty oranges to a gallon good corn whiskey. Leave two months, then pour off and add a thin syrup made of two and one-half pounds of first white sugar and one pint water boiled until it commences to thicken."

— Bluff Plantation, Cooper River

Blackberry Wine

Possibly after this recipe is published, the consumption of blackberries will be greatly increased!

Wash the berries well, and for every gallon of fruit allow two quarts of boiling water. Let the water stand on the fruit for ten or twelve hours; then strain off, pressing the pulp well.

To each gallon of the liquid add two pounds of

brown sugar. Put in a cask or jug but do not cork tightly until the fermentation is over, which will take about ten days. Then you may seal the wine up and put it away for use.

—*Mrs. Bennett*

Dixie Tea

8 cups boiling water
5 tablespoons tea leaves
Juice of 1 lemon
Juice of 6 oranges
2 cups sugar
8 cups water
1 teaspoon whole cloves

Add the boiling water to the tea, let stand five minutes and pour the tea off the leaves. Add the fruit juice and a syrup made by boiling the sugar, water and cloves to the tea. This makes about eighteen cups.

Eggnog

Julia Collier Harris sends us this recipe for eggnog. She writes that this eggnog was served in Georgia for generations at 11 o'clock each Christmas morning.

12 eggs
1 cup sugar

1 cup boiled milk
½ cup rum
1 cup brandy

Mix yolks of eggs and sugar. Then add the milk, which should be allowed to cool before adding, and the rum and brandy. Last of all, and immediately before serving, stir in gently the whites of eggs which have been beaten as stiff as possible. Do not change the proportions. This mixture has enough liquor in it for a strong man. This quantity will serve six persons one fairly tall glassful, somewhat taller than an ordinary water glass.

—*Julia Collier Harris*

This recipe is another which was not tested in the Institute kitchen! It is reasonable to assume, however, that the proportions are entirely correct.

Carolina Mint Tea

2 cups sugar
½ cup water
Grated rind of 1 orange
Juice of 6 oranges
6 glasses of very strong Orange Pekoe tea
Several sprays of mint

Boil the sugar, water and orange rind about five minutes to make a syrup. Remove from the fire, add the crushed leaves of mint and let cool.

Make the tea, strain, add the orange juice, half fill glasses with crushed ice, add tea and sweeten to taste with the mint syrup. A fresh spray of mint in each glass or a slice of orange as a garnish adds to the attractiveness of the drink.

— *Mrs. Cornelius Youmans Reamer*

Russian Tea

This tea is much better if the syrup is made the day before using. It should always be made several hours before, at least, in order to insure the delicious blend.

2 pounds sugar
1½ cups water
30 whole cloves
Grated rind of 3 oranges
2 dozen large oranges
4 large lemons
½ pound Orange Pekoe tea

Boil the sugar, water, cloves and grated orange rind ten minutes, or until it is a thick syrup. This should be done twenty-four hours before serving.

Strain the juice of the oranges and lemons, make a very black tea and add the syrup and fruit juices. Bring to the boiling point and serve very hot. This serves about fifty people — the exact amount made depending on how much water is used in making the tea and on how much juice the oranges produce.

—*Mrs. Cornelius Youmans Reamer*

Roman Punch

Another relic of the "dear, dead days" is this frozen punch.

1 quart weak tea
2 cups sugar
1 pint claret
2 tablespoons rum
1 pound glacéed cherries
Grated rind and juice of 3 lemons
Whipped cream

Mix the tea, sugar, claret and lemon rind and juice together. Freeze until of a mushy consistency. Then add the rum and the cherries cut in bits. Continue freezing. Serve topped with whipped cream.

—*Southern Cook Book*

Iced Tea à la Russe

To each goblet of cold tea add the juice of half a lemon, fill up with crushed ice and sweeten well.

A further suggestion is made that "a glass of champagne added to this makes what is called Russian Punch"!

—*Mary Leìze Simons*

Orgeat

2 quarts milk
1 stick cinnamon
$\frac{1}{4}$ pound almonds
2 tablespoons rosewater
$\frac{1}{4}$ cup sugar

Add the cinnamon to the milk and bring it gently to the boiling point. Remove the cinnamon and let the milk cool. Blanch the almonds and "pound them in a marble mortar," the directions say, but since this is not possible for most of us, chopping them very fine will do. Add the rose water to the chopped almonds and then put them into the milk, mixing well. Sweeten the milk to taste — we used one-fourth cup of sugar for a rather sweet drink — and let the milk boil for a minute or two. If it is cooked too long, the almonds will make it oily. Strain the drink through a very fine sieve or a piece of cheesecloth to remove the almonds and "serve it either cold or lukewarm in glasses with handles." We preferred it icy cold. The cinnamon, rosewater and almond flavors are so blended that it is difficult to tell just what flavor the drink really has.

INDEX

Appetizer, 14
Apple Charlotte, 65
Asparagus, 118

Beef à la Mode, 92
Beef Olives, 91
Beverages
  Blackberry Wine, 276
  Carolina Mint Tea, 278
  Dixie Tea, 277
  Eggnog, 277
  Iced Tea à la Russe, 280
  Noyan, 275
  Orange Cordial, 276
  Orgeat, 281
  Otranto Club Punch, 275
  Roman Punch, 280
  Russian Tea, 279
Breads
  Ashley Bread, 154
  Batter Bread, 155
  Breakfast Rusks, 148
  Cheese Straws, 162, 163
  Corn Batter Cakes, 145
  Corn Bread, 155–157
  Cream Muffins, 148
  Fried Corn Bread, 156
  Hoe Cake, 161
  Hominy Bread, 158
  Hominy Waffles, 146
  Light Bread Batter Bread, 164
  Old Virginia Spoon Bread, 158
  Owendow Corn Bread, 157
  Philpy, 162
  Popovers, 153
  Puff Pops, 152
  Quick Biscuits, 152
  Quick Muffins, 149
  Rice Cakes, 151
  Rice-Flour Toddles, 144
  Rice-Flour Waffles, 147
  Rice Griddle Cakes, 144
  Rice Muffins, 150
  Sally Lunn, 160
  Sweet Sally Lunn, 159
  Yeast Cakes, 164
Broccoli, 118

Cabbage, Pickled, 137
Cakes
  Alderney Cake, 208
  Angel Cake, 199

Black Cake, 179
Chocolate Cake, 181
Cocoanut Cakes, 216
Cocoanut Cream Cake, 191
Cocoanut Fruit Cake, 171
Croton Sponge Cake, 194
Fruit Cake, 168–171
Ginger Cakes, 213
Golden Cake, 196
Ground Nut Cake, 216
Jelly Cake Rolled Up, 200
Kiss Cakes, 211
Lady Baltimore Cake, 172, 174, 175
Lady Fingers, 206
Lemon Butter, 201
Lemon Cake, 187
Lemon Cocoanut Mountain, 190
Macaroons, 207
Marble Cake, 184
Marvels, 213
No-Name Cake, 192
Nut Cookies, 212
1–2–3–and–4 Cake, 193
Orange Cake, 185
Peanut Cookies, 205
Prune Cake, 195
Scripture Cake, 182
Shrewsberry Cakes, 209, 210
Silver Cake, 188
Spice Cake, 197
Sponge Cake, 198
Sugar Biscuits, 208
Sweet Wafers, 206
Washington's Prune Cake, 195
Wedding Cake, 177
White Cake, 183
White Fruit Cake, 169
Calabash, 40–42
Canapés, Cheese, 15
Candies
Benne Brittle, 220
Butterscotch, 219
Caramels, 221
Chocolate Fudge, 219
Cocoanut Fudge, 215
French Candy, 214
Peach Leather, 217, 218
Peanut Candy, 220
Carolina Pilau, 53
Catsup, Red-Pepper, 140
Cauliflower, Scalloped, 116
Cheese Toast, 60
Chicken
à la Tartare, 70
Fricassee, White, 68
Fried with Corn Cake, 66
Galantine of Chicken, 92
Mulacolong, 76
Pressed, 77
Roast Chicken, 67
Chicken, Batter for Frying, 78
Chicken à la Tartare, 70
Chicken and Rice Pilau, 52
Chicken Custard, 9
Chicken Pilau, 50–52

Chowder, Fish, 7
Cocktail Sauce for Shrimp, 15
Coloring for Icing, 222
Cooter (Terrapin) Stew, 39
Corn, Green, and Shrimp Pudding, 25
Corn, Okra, and Green Peppers, 62
Corn Pie, 62
Corn Pie, with Shrimp, 18
Crab Gumbo, 8
Crab Soup, 2
Crabs, Devilled, 30
Crabs, Stuffed, and Mushrooms, 35
Cranberries, Preserved, 134
Cucumbers, Stewed, 117
Custard, Chicken, 9

Desserts
- Ambrosia, 262
- Apple Charlotte, 256, 258
- Apple Fritters, 265
- Apple Snow, 259
- Apples, White Compote of, 259
- Blackberry Pudding, 262
- Boiled Batter Pudding, 230
- Buttermilk Custard Pie, 271
- Charlotte Russe, 238, 239, 240, 241
- Chocolate Sponge, 244
- Cocoanut Pudding, 255
- Cocoanut Tarts, 254
- Coffee Soufflé, 245
- Cottage Pudding, 251
  - Sauce for, 252
- Cream Puffs, 267
- Delmonico Peaches, 255
- Fresh Fig Ice Cream, 263
- Frozen Custard, 264
- Fruit Puffs, 267
- Fudge Sauce, 252
- Hard Sauce, 227
- Huckleberry Pudding, 228
- Ice Cream, Fresh Fig, 263
- Lemon Meringue, 248
- Lemon Pudding, 237
- Mincemeat, 269
- Orange Jelly, 241
- Pineapple Ice, 264
- Pineapple Pudding, 249
- Plum Pudding, 225, 226
- Prune Peachy, 261
- Puff Pudding, 268
- Pumpkin Pie, 270
- Queen of Puddings, 250
- Ratifia Cream, 229
- Rice Pudding, 247
- Sauce for Cottage Pudding, 252
- Snow Cream, 236
- Sponge Cake, Mince Sauce for, 249
- Strawberry Nonsense, 243
- Strawberry Shortcake, 260
- Swan's Down Cream, 234

Desserts (continued)
Sweet Marie Pudding, 228
Syllabub, 231
Tapioca Cream, 253
Transparent Pies, 269
Trifle, 235, 236
Whipped Cream, 233
Whips without Eggs, 232
White Compote of Apples, 259
Wine Jelly, 246
Wine Sauce for Sponge Cake, 249

Egg Pie, 63
Egg Pilau, 49
Egg Soup, 11
Eggs Fricassee, 61
Eggs, Stuffed, 121

Fillings and Icings
Caramel Filling, 204
Chocolate Icing, 203
Coloring for Icing, 222
Filling, 202
Lemon Butter, 201
Marshmallow Filling, 204
Fish, Baked, Tomato Sauce for, 32
Fish, Fried, 34
Fish, Sheepshead, 35
Fish Chowder, 7
Fish Soufflé, 29
French Pilau, 54–56
Fricassee, White, 68

Griddle Cakes
Corn Batter Cakes, 145
Rice-Flour Toddles, 144
Rice Griddle Cakes, 144
Gumbo, New Orleans, 5
Gumbo, with Crabs or Shrimp, 8

Ham
Barbecued, 93
Virginia, 97
Hominy, Shrimps with, 20
Hopping John, 58

Icings. *See* Fillings and Icings

Jambalayah, 56
Jelly, Blackberry, 272

Liver, Larded, 96

Macaroni Pie, 60
Macaroni, Potage au, 64
Meats, 89–100
Beef à la Mode, 92
Beef Olives, 91
Ham, Barbecued, 93
Ham, Virginia, 97
Liver, Larded, 96
Mutton Hash, 97
Oxtail, Stewed, 90
Rice Pie, 100
Scrapple, 95
Veal, Smothered, 94
Veal or Venison Patty, 98

Muffins
Breakfast Rusks, 148
Cream Muffins, 148
Quick Muffins, 149
Rice Muffins, 150
Mulacolong, 76
Mushrooms, Stuffed Crabs and, 35
Mutton Hash, 97

Okra, 119
Okra, Corn and Green Peppers, 62
Okra Pilau, 46–48
Oxtail, Stewed, 90
Oyster Soup, 10, 12
Oysters à la Newburg, 36
Oysters in Bread Cases, 37

Peaches, Brandy, 135, 136
Peas and Rice Pilau, 59
Pecan Turkey Stuffing, 73
Pickle, Green Tomato, 138, 139
Pie, Sweet Potato, 112
Pigeon Pie, 75
Pilaus
Carolina Pilau, 53
Carolina Tomato Pilau, 48
Chicken and Rice Pilau, 52
Chicken Pilau, 50–52
Egg Pilau, 49
French Pilau, 54–56
Okra Pilau, 46–48
Peas and Rice Pilau, 59
Roast Squab with Rice Pilau, 45
Shrimp Pilau, 24
Pine Bark Stew, 33
Pudding, Sweet Potato, 109, 110, 111, 113
Pumpkin, Ophir Cooked, 120
Pumpkin Chips, 141, 142

Red-Pepper Catsup, 140
Red Rice, 57
Rice Dishes
Carolina Pilau, 53
Carolina Tomato Pilau, 48
Chicken and Rice Pilau, 52
Chicken Pilau, 50–52
Egg Pilau, 49
French Pilau, 54–56
Hopping John, 58
Jambalayah, 56
Okra Pilau, 46–48
Peas and Rice Pilau, 59
Red Rice, 57
Rice, Boiled, 114, 115
Rice Croquettes, 115, 116
Roast Squab with Rice Pilau, 45
Roast Chicken, 67

Salad Dressing, 132–133
for Fruit, 133
Salads
Apple Salad, Cinnamon, 123

Asparagus Salad, 129
Cream Cheese Salad, 127
Grapefruit Aspic with Almonds, 122
Nut Salad, 130
Philadelphia Cream Cheese Salad, 128
Royal Salad, 131
Salmon Salad, 132
Tomato and Cheese Aspic, 124, 125, 126
Tomato Aspic Jelly, 123
Tomato Salad, 131
Sandwiches, Russian, 134
Sauce, Tomato, for Baked Fish, 32
Scrapple, 95
Shad, Baked, 31
Sheepshead, 35
Shrimp
Baked Shrimps and Tomatoes, 25
Cocktail Sauce for, 15
Corn Pie with, 18
Green Corn and Shrimp Pudding, 25
Shrimp Gumbo, 8
Shrimp Paste, 26–29
Shrimp Patties, 19
Shrimp Pie, 21–24
Shrimp Pilau, 24
Shrimp Soup, 4, 5
Shrimps with Hominy, 20
Soufflé, Fish, 29
Soups, 1–14
Crab Soup, 2
Chicken Custard Soup, 9
Egg Soup, 11
Fish Chowder, 7
Gumbo, New Orleans, 5
Gumbo with Crabs or Shrimp, 8
Oyster Soup, 10, 12
Potage au Macaroni, 64
Shrimp Soup, 4, 5
Terrapin Soup, 38
Turnip Soup, 7
Squab, Roast, with Rice Pilau, 45
Stew, Cooter (Terrapin), 39
Stuffings
Chicken Dressing, 84
Chicken Dressing, Sally Washington's, 86
Corn Bread Dressing, Aiken County, 83
Corn Bread Stuffing, 87
Oyster Stuffing, 84
Peanut Dressing, 87
Pecan Turkey Stuffing, 73
Veal and Chestnut Stuffing, 85
Sweet Potato Croquettes, 103
Sweet Potato Marshmallow Pudding, 113
Sweet Potato Pears, 111
Sweet Potato Pie, 112
Sweet Potato Pone, 104–108

Sweet Potato Pudding, 109, 110
Sweet Potato Pudding, Lemon, 111
Sweet Potatoes Margherita, 103
Sweet Potatoes with Apple, 114

Terrapin, 38
Terrapin Soup, 38
Terrapin (Cooter) Stew 39
Calabash, 40–42
Tomato, Green, Pickle, 138, 139
Tomato Pilau, 48
Tomato Sauce for Baked Fish, 32
Tomatoes, Baked Shrimps and, 25
Turkey Hash, 71
Turkey Stuffing, Pecan, 73
Turnip Soup, 7

Veal, Smothered, 94
Veal or Venison Patty, 98

Waffles, Hominy, 146
Waffles, Rice-Flour, 147

Betsy + Chris,

Best wishes from us
to you, wherever you may
be. Happy cooking!

Karen & Mike
Nov. 1976